KU-432-238

Table A Scientific terms and concepts introduced or developed in Block 1A

accumulated stress   30

active rifting (model)   15

adiabatic temperature gradient   13

back-arc spreading   56

Basin and Range Province   58

boundary layer model (for the lithosphere)   8

breakaway zone (in lithosphere rifting)   61

brittle deformation   29

Cadomian terrane   81

conductive geotherm   11

convective (adiabatic) geotherm   11

core complex   62

critical stress   36

decompression (of mantle material)   12

detachment zone (in lithosphere rifting)   62

displaced (exotic) terrane   68

ductile flow   29

dynamic viscosity (η)   28

elastic lithosphere   7

geosynclines   48

inelastic (plastic) deformation   29

instantaneous strength   28

island arc accretion   57

kimberlite pipes   21

leaky transform fault   51

listric fault   61

marginal (back-arc) basins   56

mechanical boundary layer   9

ocean depth–time constant (K)   7

passive rifting (model)   15

plate model (for the lithosphere)   8

plate movement vectors   48

plateau uplift force (F_{PU})   37

pure shear (McKenzie) model   61

reduced heat flow   17

refractory mantle   26

rheological boundaries   34

rheology   6, 29

roll-over   61

seismic wave attenuation   24

simple shear (Wernicke) model   61

SS phase (of shear waves)   24

strain hardening   42

strain rate   31

strain softening   41

stress amplification   34

stretching factor (β)   22

tectonic subsidence/uplift   62, 63

tectosphere   26

terrane   65

Tethyan faunal province   68

thermal boundary layer   10

thermal relaxation   41

thermal subsidence/uplift   22

thermal subsidence history   22

thermal time constant (C)   7

transient geotherm   41

transpression   51

transtension   51

Variscan Front   73

viscoelastic lithosphere   30

whole lithosphere failure (WLF)   30

4

OBJECTIVES FOR BLOCK 1A

When you have completed Block 1A, you should be able to:

1 Define and use, or recognize correct definitions and applications of, each of the terms listed in Table A.

2 Explain how the thickness and heat flow of the oceanic lithosphere may be integrated in terms of age and ocean bathymetry.

3 Demonstrate how the oceanic lithosphere may be interpreted in terms of a rigid mechanical boundary layer overlying a thermal boundary layer and a plastic asthenosphere.

4 Give an account of the thermal structure of oceanic lithosphere in relation to boundary layer models: (a) below stable 'old' (>60 Ma) lithosphere; and (b) below an ocean ridge.

5 Distinguish the major contributions to heat flow through continental lithosphere, and explain how these contributions may be used to calculate thermal gradients within such lithosphere.

6 Explain how (a) continental heat flow measurements and (b) thermal subsidence histories may be used to make an approximate estimate of the thickness of the continental lithosphere.

7 Outline and account for the distribution and characteristics of mantle low velocity zones in terms of possible variations in the physical state and chemical composition of the lithospheric mantle and asthenosphere.

8 Explain the physical factors responsible for the contrasted rheologies of the lithosphere and asthenosphere, and how these relate to brittle and ductile deformation within the lithosphere.

9 Write an account of the concept of the viscoelastic lithosphere and how this may be used to interpret whole lithosphere failure (WLF).

10 Explain how the strain rates of individual minerals present within the crust and lithospheric mantle and geothermal gradient data may be used to interpret the site and timing of WLF.

11 From data concerning critical stress and heat flow, comment on the stress necessary for WLF under compressional and extensional regimes.

12 Relate the concepts of critical stress and heat flow to data for varied natural geological situations such as continental lithosphere experiencing extension or compression.

13 Use stress and heat flow data to account for the concepts of strain softening and strain hardening during deformation of continental lithosphere.

14 Write an account of the major geological features of divergent, convergent and conservative plate boundaries, and explain why (a) plate boundaries should be studied in terms of an absolute frame of reference and (b) some plate boundaries show characteristics of more than one of these types.

15 Distinguish between (a) different types and (b) the stability of plate triple junctions.

16 Given an interpretation of the recent geological stress history of an area, write an account of a possible plate tectonic evolution in terms of the principles identified in Objectives 14 and 15.

17 Summarize the geological characteristics of marginal basins, and explain how their formation may be related to processes adjacent to major ocean basins.

18 From geological data for an active continental extensional province, explain how you would discriminate between contrasted (simple and pure shear) tectonic models to account for the style of extension.

19   From geological and geophysical data, (a) write an account of the concept of terrane accretion, and (b) explain how this process has been responsible for continental modification and growth.

20   From appropriate data, write a brief summary of selected aspects of the geological history of the British Isles in terms of the plate tectonic processes identified in Objectives 14–19.

1   INTRODUCTION AND STUDY COMMENT

In *Understanding the Continents,* we try to explain the formation, modification and evolution of the Earth's continental crust. The crust forms the 'lid' on the lithosphere, and to explain continental processes we need to understand the properties and behaviour of the continental lithosphere. In Block 1, we therefore describe the properties and plate tectonic behaviour of the lithosphere on a global scale (1A), and then examine regional geological and geophysical data for Britain in terms of crustal evolution by collision of contrasted lithospheric blocks (1B).

In Block 1A, we therefore look first at how the lithosphere is defined, and then summarize its variations in thickness, thermal structure, strength and rheology (Section 2). These properties enable you to revise and extend your knowledge of the plate tectonic processes occurring at plate boundaries (Section 3). This is achieved by introducing case studies (the western USA, for example) which demonstrate the important role of widespread migration of contrasted continental (and oceanic) blocks or terranes in continental evolution, and Block 1A concludes with a summary of the plate tectonic history of the British Isles (Section 3.4).

In addition to the printed text, Block 1A has two video cassette sequences; *Extensional Tectonics* (an S338 programme) and *Extension in the North Sea* (both on videocassette VC 271), which you should view at the points indicated in the text. The notes relating to these videos are included within this text.

2   WHAT IS THE LITHOSPHERE?

Plate tectonics is a global model accounting for a wide range of observations on the behaviour of the Earth's outer skin. This skin, or lithosphere (rock layer) is the crucial element in plate tectonics, and we think of the lithosphere in terms of a rigid layer, about 100 km or more in thickness, which comprises the continental and oceanic crusts and uppermost mantle of the Earth. The lithosphere is divided into 'plates' which move as discrete units relative to each other at extensional, compressional and conservative plate boundaries (Figure 2.1).

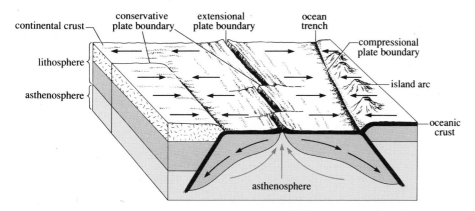

Figure 2.1   Simplified block model showing the three different types of plate boundary in relation to the directions of movement (arrows) of material in the rigid lithosphere (above) and weaker asthenosphere (below).

6

As you know, many geological processes are the direct or indirect result of inter-actions at the boundaries between lithospheric plates, and this means that under-standing the lithosphere is of fundamental importance in modern Earth sciences. What is less well appreciated is that the nature of these processes is controlled by the mechanical structure and strength of the plates. As you will find in this Course, sedimentary basins may form where plates are weakened and stretch under tension, and areally extensive high-grade metamorphic terrains develop where strong, rigid plates interact under compression. An important influence on plate behaviour is the thermal state of the lithosphere; hot lithosphere will be weaker than cold litho-sphere, and vice versa. Plate movements and plate boundary processes are the result of internal convection caused by the cooling of the Earth. Heat is lost at the surface by conduction through the lithosphere, while the results of internal convective processes are exposed to the surface at plate boundaries. *The distinction between the lithosphere and the asthenosphere is that the lithosphere is an outer, rigid, heat con-ducting layer, while the asthenosphere is an underlying weaker layer that is mobile and convecting; the boundary between the two is thus, to a first approximation, the boundary between a rigid conducting layer and a mobile convecting layer.*

This type of distinction based on fundamental properties tells us little about the thickness of the lithosphere or its internal structure. You are probably familiar with vague statements such as 'about 100 km thick under the oceans and 200 km beneath the continents'. Attempts to determine the thickness of the lithosphere geophysi-cally have been fraught with difficulty but are now reaching some consensus, as you will see from the results in Section 2.1. You will also realize that the lithosphere is stratified, with different chemical and mineralogical compositions, and hence different physical properties in the upper crust, lower crust and upper mantle. Consequently, the thermal structure, density and **rheology** (i.e. deformation behaviour) are unlikely to be constant throughout. Variations of each of these properties will have a profound effect on surface geological processes, a subject that we introduce in Section 2.2. Moreover, the concept of highly rigid plates is also questionable when viewed over geological time-scales longer than those of the iso-static readjustment processes (10^4–10^5 years) that were originally used to define the rigid lithosphere. Even the most rigid material will deform if the applied forces are strong enough and operate for long enough! So remember as you read on that the lithosphere is just *more* rigid than the asthenosphere.

Finally, there is the strong contrast between the relatively permanent, low density continental crust and the transient, higher density, oceanic crust, which is created and subducted on a geologically brief time-scale. The continents preserve a geologi-cal history going back approximately 4 000 Ma, whereas oceanic crustal lifespans reach a maximum of 180 Ma. This, in turn, raises questions about the much more extensive mantle portions of the oceanic and continental lithospheres; like their crustal counterparts, is the former recycled and the latter permanent? Are, therefore, their chemical and physical characteristics considerably different? Is this another fundamental determinant of surface geological and tectonic processes — especially given that most of the Earth's larger plates have thicker continental and thinner oceanic portions? These are some of the key questions we address throughout this Course. We start by considering the geophysical evidence for lithosphere thickness, its thermal structure and deformation behaviour, as a prelude to examining (in Section 3) some case studies of lithospheric processes which will be developed in more detail in subsequent Blocks. Block 1B introduces geophysical evidence for the structure of the lithosphere in the UK, again as a means of illustrating some of the global tectonic processes that are a central theme of this Course.

2.1 LITHOSPHERE THICKNESS AND THERMAL STRUCTURE

A fundamental property of the Earth's lithosphere is that it bends when a sufficient load is applied to the surface; for example, by formation of an ice cap or a young volcano. In these cases, the lithosphere shows *elastic* properties, because, if the load is removed, the lithosphere returns to its former shape, just like an elastic band. Such observations of *isostatic rebound,* reflecting elastic behaviour in a relatively strong layer overlying a weaker zone where material deforms plastically (i.e. permanently), led geophysicists of the early 1900s to propose the concept of an **elastic lithosphere**. The weaker, plastic zone beneath, which deforms to accommodate bending of the lithosphere, is the asthenosphere. While the details need not concern us here, the earliest estimates of lithosphere thickness were based on analysis of gravitational data, coupled with the principle of isostasy, applied to large mountains. This method led to estimations of the thickness of the rigid layer capable of supporting the forces due to such mountains for geologically long periods of time. In this way, various estimates between 50 km and 100 km for the thickness of the elastic lithosphere were derived for continental areas. These estimates turned out to be rather low because, as you will see in Section 2.2, the lithosphere is not such a *perfectly* elastic layer as first thought.

Most recently, it was realized that the thickness of the lithosphere (z) depends on the conductive temperature gradient through the plate ($\Delta T/z$), a high thermal gradient reflecting a thin lithosphere and vice versa (Figure 2.2). This assumes that the lithosphere–athenosphere boundary is at a more-or-less fixed temperature, independent of depth. *Thus an accepted definition is that the lithosphere is a rigid, thermally conducting boundary layer around the Earth.* While this is also good to a first approximation, consideration of temperature distributions near the base of the lithosphere led to a revised definition as we shall see in Section 2.1.1. Much more progress has been made during the last 20–30 years using combinations of different geophysical methods and petrological data, though definitions of thickness still do not all agree. We start with the oceanic lithosphere, which is much simpler and more fully understood than that of continental areas.

2.1.1 Oceanic lithosphere

Much research has been focused on the correlations between oceanic heat flow, lithospheric age and ocean bathymetry, and you may recall from earlier courses that oceanic heat flow (q) decreases as the square root of age increases:

$$q \propto \frac{1}{t^{0.5}}, \text{ or } q \propto t^{-0.5}, \text{ or } q = Ct^{-0.5} \tag{2.1}$$

where t is time (i.e. age), and C is the **thermal time constant** governing the decay of heat flow.

Much more data exist on ocean bathymetry than on heat flow, so a common form of analysis involves plotting ocean depth (instead of heat flow) against the square root of age (see Figure 2.3). Again a square root correlation is found, but this time because ocean depth (d) increases as time (t) increases:

$$d \propto t^{0.5}, \text{ or change in depth, } \Delta d = Kt^{0.5} \tag{2.2}$$

where K is the **ocean depth–time constant**.

> **ITQ 2.1** Use the linear part of the graph in Figure 2.3 to calculate the ocean depth–time constant, K. What is the significance of the number you have just calculated?

Figure 2.3 shows that the linear relationship holds out to an age of about 60 Ma ($t^{0.5} = 7.7$), and we shall examine the older parts of the heat flow–depth–time relationship shortly. First, equations 2.1 and 2.2 prove that, for ages less than 60 Ma, ocean depth is, quite simply, inversely related to heat flow, which, of course, is itself determined by the temperature distribution within the lithosphere.

> So, if the oceans get deeper as heat flow and lithosphere temperatures decrease, what is likely to be the principal mechanism involved?

It is likely that as the lithosphere cools, so it *contracts,* becomes more dense, and therefore subsides as it moves away from the region of active ridge volcanism. As you can see from the square root relationship (cf. ITQ 2.1 answer) the lithosphere contracts and cools ever more slowly as it gets older — the same increment of depth and decrement of heat flow occurs in the interval 1–4 Ma as, for example, in the interval 36–49 Ma. Most important from our point of view, the greater the height,

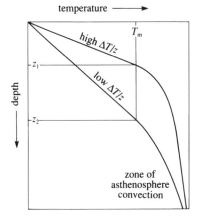

Figure 2.2 Schematic illustration of relationship between the thickness of the lithosphere (z_1, and z_2) and temperature gradient ($\Delta T/z$) showing that a high temperature gradient leads to a thin lithosphere and vice versa. In this illustration, the base of the two conducting layers is defined by the same temperature T_m; the much slower rate of temperature increase with depth in the underlying mantle is because of convection.

$$K = \frac{\Delta d}{t^{0.5}} = \Delta d \, t^{-0.5}$$
$$= 4500/12.8 = 350 \text{m} M_a^{-0.5}$$

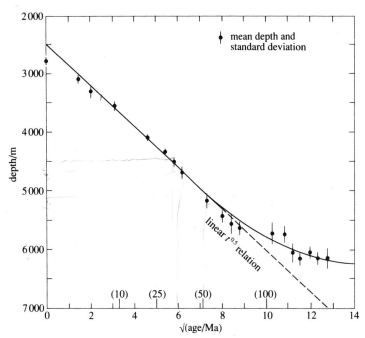

Figure 2.3 Plot of mean depth in the North Pacific against the square root of age. Numbers in brackets give real ages in Ma for comparison.

or thickness, of the contracting lithosphere column, the greater will be the depth increment in a given $t^{0.5}$ interval, and so the greater will be the proportionality constant K. It is therefore possible to use values of K determined by observations of age and bathymetry to calculate the thickness of the cooling lithosphere. The calculations are extremely complex because many variables are involved, but a good fit for all parameters is obtained for a cooling lithosphere with an overall thickness of about 125 km.

So roughly what percentage contraction in a vertical sense does the oceanic lithosphere undergo in its first 60 Ma?

From Figure 2.3, the contraction is 2.7 km, and if this occurs in a 125 km thick lithosphere there is roughly 2% contraction. Although this may be small, it makes a lot of difference to the depth of the ocean basins! Now you may recall from an earlier course that two possible models have been proposed to explain the quantitative relationships expressed in equations 2.1 and 2.2. These are illustrated in simple terms in Figure 2.4. The only difference is in the way they describe the base of the lithosphere. In the **plate model** (Figure 2.4a), the plate thickness is constant (125 km) and the temperature remains fixed at the base, so *cooling within the plate* away from the ridge accounts for decreasing surface heat flow and contraction. In the **boundary layer model** (Figure 2.4b), a constant heat flow occurs at the base of the plate, which means that the *plate thickness* must increase (towards 125 km) with age to reduce surface heat flow. Note that surface heat flow (q) varies with the temperature gradient ($\Delta T/z$) within the contracting lithosphere. So, on the boundary layer model, where ΔT across the lithosphere is also almost constant, the greater the lithosphere thickness (z), the smaller will be the surface heat flow (q).

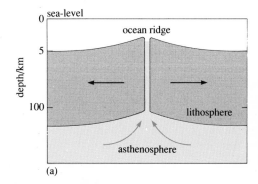
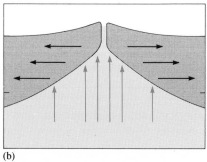

Figure 2.4 Schematic sections through oceanic lithosphere according to: (a) the plate model, in which the oceanic lithosphere thickness stays constant during spreading and the basal temperature is fixed; and (b) the boundary layer model, in which oceanic lithosphere thickens during spreading and heat flow from the base is constant.

The plate and boundary layer models really amount to two different ways of describing the same temperature and heat flow distribution — in other words, both are a good approximation — because the thermal structure beneath the ocean basins is more-or-less identical on both models (Figure 2.5). A best estimate for the basal temperature on the plate model is 1 350 °C, roughly the temperature at which mantle peridotite changes from elastic to plastic behaviour under the old ocean basins. We shall be discussing this important basal temperature in much more detail in a moment. First, notice that the decrease with $t^{0.5}$ of heat flow and near-surface temperatures in a lithosphere with a uniform basal temperature (the plate model) implies that the isotherms are gradually becoming more horizontal away from the ridge (Figure 2.5). This reflects a trend towards a uniform vertical temperature gradient (1 350/125 = 10.8 °C km^{-1}) far from the ridge.

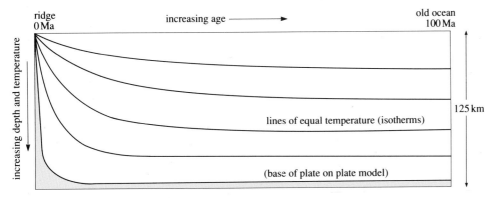

Figure 2.5 Schematic illustration of probable thermal structure beneath ocean basins showing how isotherms within the upper mantle become deeper with increasing distance from the ridge.

But surely the heat flow–bathymetry–age correlation dictates that the lithosphere continues to cool (plate model) and thicken (boundary layer model)? This is not so beyond 60 Ma (Figure 2.3), where we see that the oceans become less deep than predicted by the $t^{0.5}$ relationship.

> **ITQ 2.2** What must the flattening out of ocean bathymetry beyond 60 Ma imply for (a) the overall density of the lithosphere, and (b) lithosphere temperatures, in particular the nature of the isotherms in old parts of the oceanic lithosphere?

So, oceanic lithosphere older than 60 Ma must be less dense than predicted by the $t^{0.5}$ model, implying higher temperatures. To account for this observation, it is believed that there is a convective replacement of cold material by hotter material beneath the base of an old plate and that this maintains the basal isotherm of 1 350 °C at 125 km depth. Thus, the thermal structure of the plate must be tending towards uniform conditions, with invariant isotherms. Certainly the *rate* of thermal decay, governed by the time constants C (thermal time constant) and K (ocean depth–time constant), must decrease much less rapidly after 60 Ma to account for the bathymetry in Figure 2.3.

We can now examine the significance of basal lithosphere temperatures in more detail, and this leads us back to the rigid-plate definition of the lithosphere. Here, the concept of the lithosphere as a *boundary layer,* forming the rigid skin of the Earth and overlying a plastic asthenosphere, becomes useful. Consideration of the physical behaviour of these two layers has led to the recognition that there must be a transition zone between them where the material is neither rigid (unyielding) nor plastic (ductile and yielding). It is envisaged that this transition zone will be characterized by *viscous* behaviour, so that it will be able to flow and thus be yielding, like the plastic layer beneath, but will nevertheless retain a strong resistance to flow (like cold treacle, which is a viscous liquid). (Note that we shall be looking at the viscosity and deformation behaviour of the lithosphere more rigorously in Section 2.2). Because of its rigid, mechanical (in the sense of stress-resisting) behaviour, the outermost lithosphere layer has become known as the **mechanical boundary layer**.

This layer lies between the surface and the depth to an isotherm (say at T_1) that represents the transition from rigid (above) to viscous (below) behaviour. This isotherm, and a deeper one (at T_2), define the limits of the transitional layer, which is connected physically to the mechanical layer and moves along with it, yet which is capable of independent internal convective movement. It has become known as the **thermal boundary layer** (Figure 2.6a).

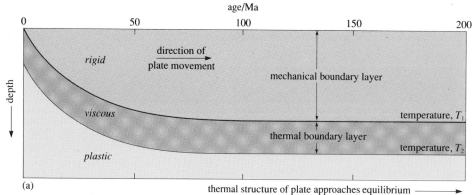

Figure 2.6 (a) Schematic diagram showing the division of the oceanic plate into a rigid mechanical layer and a viscous thermal boundary layer. Heat flow at the base of both boundary layers is constant across the diagram according to the boundary layer model. This illustration is also consistent with the bathymetric evidence that the base of the oceanic plate tends towards a uniform temperature and depth after 60 Ma. The interfaces between the layers shown are *almost* isothermal; the reason why they are not quite isothermal will become clear from Figures 2.9 and 2.10.

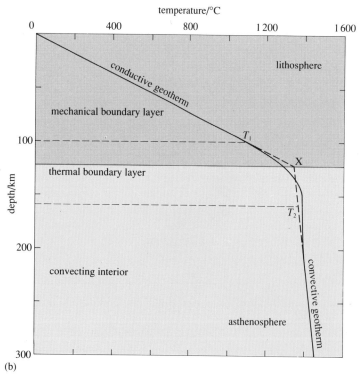

Figure 2.6 (b) Geotherm for old oceanic lithosphere and asthenosphere illustrating the definitions of the mechanical and thermal boundary layers in terms of basal isotherms at temperatures T_1 and T_2. The best theoretical definition of plate thickness is the depth at which the projected conductive and convective parts of the geotherm meet, at X. Note that the convective part of the geotherm steepens just before meeting the upper, conductive geotherm because heat builds up, due to convective rise from beneath, as viscosity increases near the base of the thermal boundary layer. Similarly, because of its lower viscosity compared with the mechanical boundary layer, the temperature decreases at the top of the thermal boundary layer.

The thickness of the mechanical boundary layer increases with age out to 60 Ma, while the thermal boundary layer maintains roughly equal thickness. This is because isotherms at the critical temperatures T_1 and T_2 both become deeper on the boundary layer model as the plate cools, until a constant depth is reached after 60 Ma. You might have noticed the divergence between the plate and boundary layer models in terms of the physical behaviour of the lithosphere beneath ridge zones. Comparison of Figures 2.4 and 2.6a suggests that, on the plate model, the lithosphere must include both boundary layers and some of the plastically deforming region beneath! The boundary layer model therefore seems to provide the best picture of oceanic lithosphere *deformation* behaviour.

Because the thermal boundary layer represents the transitional region between the heat conducting mechanical boundary layer above and the convecting mantle beneath, not surprisingly the variation of temperature with depth, or *geotherm,* is curved across this region, as you can see in Figure 2.6b (cf. Figure 2.2). The degree of curvature is directly related to the thickness of the thermal boundary layer, which itself depends on the viscosity of this transitional region. The more viscous the material is in this region, the thicker will be the thermal boundary layer. A simple and widely accepted definition of the thickness of the lithospheric plate is the depth at which the upwards projected **convective geotherm** intersects the downwards projected **conductive geotherm** — point X in Figure 2.6b. Here the temperature is 1 350 °C and the depth, 125 km: these are the generally accepted values for old oceanic plate (i.e. > 60 Ma, though some authors prefer 1 335 °C and depths nearer 100 km). *So the lithospheric plate is defined as the rigid mechanical boundary layer plus the upper part of the thermal boundary layer which is capable of moving independently, yet is attached by viscous drag to the rigid layer above.* This definition is the one we shall adopt in this Course because it is based on the difference in physical properties of the lithosphere and asthenosphere; as you will appreciate by comparing Figures 2.4 and 2.6a, it is more consistent with the boundary layer model for the oceanic lithosphere.

Finally in this analysis of ocean lithosphere, what about the thermal structure of ocean ridges? One of the most illuminating geophysical discoveries in recent years, on a global scale, comes from the use of satellites that use radar for precise distance measurements: these are known as the Seasat radar altimeters. Such satellites are able to map large-scale anomalies in the gravity field of the Earth, which are observed as sea-level heights above and below the mean surface corresponding, respectively, to negative and positive gravity anomalies. These anomalies are thought to be a direct reflection of underlying mantle convection. For example, a rising (warm, less dense) jet in the mantle will give a gravity low, whereas a descending (cold, more dense) one will be associated with a gravity high. Although many rising and sinking jets of hotter and colder material have now been found in oceanic areas, there is no obvious association with spreading ridges, which, in some places, lie above regions with a gravity high where the mantle below is actually sinking! While this is not a course about mantle convection, these observations do reveal an important and relevant fact — that rising plumes of hot material from the deep mantle are *not* necessary precursors for igneous activity at spreading ridges as was thought until the early 1980s (Figure 2.7). If the temperature of the sublithospheric mantle beneath ocean ridges is no different from that of normal mantle, could this mean that the associated lithosphere is no thinner than elsewhere under the ocean basins? Remember that this was a feature of the plate model (Figure 2.4a) in which we have a fixed isotherm at the base and the thermal gradient *within* the lithosphere itself must differ in high and low heat flow zones.

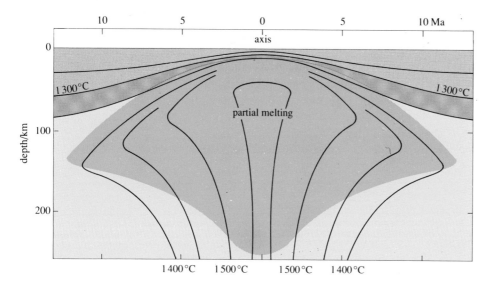

Figure 2.7 Summary of the thermal structure of an active spreading ridge that coincides with a rising hot plume in the mantle. As explained in the text (cf. Figure 2.10), today it is considered that such plumes are not necessary precursors for the development of spreading ridges and that extensional processes alone may suffice.

To understand how this horizontal isotherm may arise, we need to consider the forces that operate at ocean ridges.

Can you recall what the overall stress regime is at spreading ridges?

Oceanic spreading ridges are regions of *net lithosphere extension*. This is shown by extensional earthquake fault plane solutions and by the evidence for spreading from magnetic stripes; it is also a logical consequence of deductions about the major forces that operate on oceanic plates. These are illustrated in Figure 2.8 and are summarized in Table 2.1. You may recall a discussion of these forces from a second-level course, where we concluded that oceanic spreading is primarily controlled by the balance of forces acting on the down-going subducted slab: F_{SP} which pulls the plate, and F_{SR} and F_{CR} which provide lesser resistive forces, due mainly to friction. However, these are not the only plate-driving forces, because plates with little or no connection to subducting slabs also move, albeit more slowly, probably under the influence of pushing or sliding from ridges (F_{RP}) and hot spots (F_{HS}). These forces would be balanced by mantle drag (F_{DF}, F_{CD}) and transform fault resistance (F_{TF}). Overall, then, the oceanic lithosphere is pulled from subduction zones, and again this creates tension across the plate and at spreading ridges. If the shallow mantle beneath ocean ridges is undergoing extension, it is being **decompressed**.

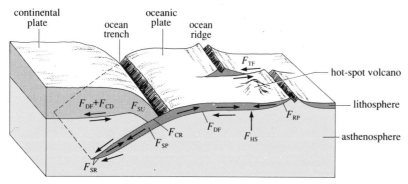

Figure 2.8 Summary of possible forces acting on lithospheric plates — see Table 2.1 for names and details of forces.

Table 2.1 Summary of possible forces acting on lithospheric plates

Force	Symbol	Where force operates	Driving or resistive force
Drag (Force)	F_{DF}	bottom surface of plates	either*
Continental Drag	F_{CD}	bottom of continental plates	resistive
Ridge Push	F_{RP}	constructive margins	driving
Transform Fault	F_{TF}	conservative margins	resistive
Slab Pull	F_{SP}	destructive margins	driving
Slab Resistance	F_{SR}	destructive margins	resistive
Collision Resistance	F_{CR}	destructive margins	resistive
Suction	F_{SU}	destructive margins	driving
Hot Spot	F_{HS}	bottom surface of plates	driving

*If the lithosphere is being carried along by asthenosphere convection, F_{DF} may be a driving force; if the lithosphere is either pulled independently from destructive margins, or pushed from constructive margins, F_{DF} may be a resistive force.

> What will this do to its density?

The density will decrease, and so the hot material will rise towards the surface. The material will rise rapidly, probably by tens of metres a day beneath ocean ridges, and will therefore carry heat energy with it.

> But what happens to the *temperature* of decompressed material, if it were to gain or lose no heat energy?

As the atoms become less closely compressed, so the temperature falls, and the particular variation of temperature with pressure, or depth in the Earth, for a given material neither gaining nor losing heat is the **adiabatic temperature gradient**, or *adiabat*. (This is a concept you will have met in previous courses, perhaps in relation to gases. For example, the temperature of the air in a bicycle pump increases when squashed.) Remember that the heat content of the material is unchanged if it follows the adiabatic pressure–temperature curve. Indeed, the temperature increase with depth in the asthenosphere shown in Figures 2.2 and 2.6b is the adiabatic temperature gradient for mantle materials: it is about $0.6\,°C\,km^{-1}$ in the upper mantle (Figure 2.6b), but may be as large as $1\,°C\,km^{-1}$ at greater depth. The adiabat is the temperature gradient that is produced within material that is freely convecting. If extra heat is added, convection becomes more rapid, but if the temperature gradient falls below that of the adiabat, convection will cease.

> **ITQ 2.3** Figure 2.9 shows the normal oceanic lithosphere geotherm (from Figure 2.6b) together with the dry solidus, where a partial melt must exist for mantle peridotite. (In practice, some volatiles will be present, which will lower the melting temperature, but for simplicity, we will assume the dry solidus here.) Also shown, dashed, is the continuation of the mantle adiabat towards the surface.
>
> (a) If material rises adiabatically from the lithosphere–asthenosphere boundary, at what minimum temperature and depth must it have become partially molten?
>
> (b) In broad terms, what kind of magma do you think will be produced?
>
> (c) What, then, are the likely consequences of the extensional stress regime at ocean ridge zones for the overall thermal structure of the lithosphere and degree of partial melting immediately beneath the ridge axis?

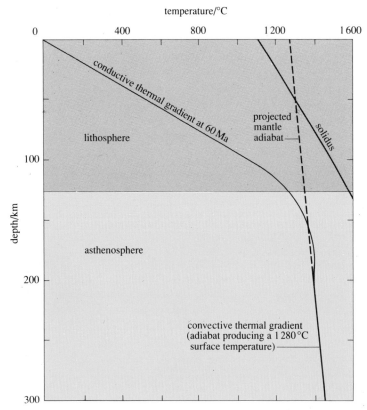

Figure 2.9 Normal ocean lithosphere geotherm in relation to the dry solidus for mantle peridotite (for use with ITQ 2.3).

So, extension at ocean ridges can allow asthenospheric material to rise under adiabatic conditions; that which reaches levels shallower than 50 km will undergo partial melting. (Note that this requires ideal circumstances of rapid ascent and limited cooling; if there is heat loss to the surroundings, then any melt produced above 50 km depth may freeze before reaching the surface.) The ideal process is illustrated in Figure 2.10 where the uppermost 50 km of material is extensively molten, and there are trace amounts of melt beneath due to partial melting in the presence of volatiles (e.g. water, CO_2) at temperatures below the dry solidus. All this melt, being basaltic, is of lower density than the residual 'depleted' peridotite solid; it is therefore buoyant, and rises to form the top 8 km or so — the ocean crust. Some of the melt may appear in volcanic activity at the surface (e.g. submarine pillow lavas), while the remainder forms intrusions (dykes and magma chambers) that crystallize as spreading takes place.

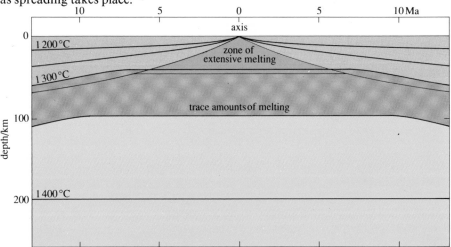

Figure 2.10 Summary of the thermal structure of an active spreading ridge in which the ridge is a passive feature created by adiabatic uprise of asthenosphere material as a result of tensional stresses where two plates are separating. The dark pink area indicates the zone in which partial melting can occur at temperatures above the dry solidus for mantle peridotite (cf. Figure 2.9).

If asthenopheric material rises adiabatically from 100 km depth towards the surface (i.e. starting at a temperature of c. 1 350 °C — Figures 2.9 and 2.10), then it may arrive having cooled only along the adiabat. In other words, material with a heat content appropriate to 100 km depth is now located close to the surface. In the extreme case where this material is erupted at a temperature close to 1 280 °C (the adiabatic temperature at the surface — Figure 2.9), the geotherm will have no conductive portion because material close to the adiabat (1 280 °C at the surface) is being erupted. In terms of our definition of lithosphere thickness as the intersection depth of the projected conductive and convective geotherms (Figure 2.6b), this means that the plate has a zero thickness over an erupting ridge. As crystallization occurs, a thin mechanical boundary layer starts to grow and thicken rapidly away from the ridge, so that the plate extends to about 35 km depth — the crust and the topmost mantle — after 5 Ma (Figure 2.10). At this stage, a conductive geotherm drawn to meet the adiabat at 35 km depth would still intersect the partial melt field, though relatively little melt will be present, most having been extracted to form ocean crust at the ridge 5 Ma earlier.

After 10 Ma, the isotherms are falling slightly less rapidly, and the plate thickness (defined, remember, as the intersection between the conductive geotherm and the adiabat, i.e. the projected convective thermal gradient) will have reached 60 km. At this point, you should draw a line from the origin in Figure 2.9 to intersect the adiabat at a depth of 60 km and label it '10 Ma old plate'; the basal temperature is close to 1 300 °C as indicated in Figure 2.10. Thereafter, the plate will continue to thicken (cf. Figure 2.6a) reaching its full 125 km thickness at 60 Ma age. Notice how the 'isotherms' T_1 and T_2 in Figure 2.6a need to be corrected for the adiabatic thermal gradient. For example, it follows from Figure 2.9 that T_2 (bottom of thermal boundary layer) increases in temperature from about 1 300 °C beneath the ridge to about 1 370 °C beneath the old oceanic plate. So, on the boundary layer model for the oceanic lithosphere, the thickness of the lithosphere increases from zero at an erupting ridge to 35 km after 5 Ma, 60 km after 10 Ma, and eventually reaches a constant depth of 125 km after 60 Ma.

Finally, perhaps the most important feature of Figure 2.10 is the presence of a horizontal isotherm, shown as 1 400 °C at 200 km depth. As asthenospheric mantle rises adiabatically, thermal disturbances will be found *only where the otherwise conductive layer is interrupted by hot ascending material*. Interestingly, the thermal structure of the upper mantle, even as shallow as 125 km, is probably insensitive and immaterial to the formation of ocean ridges! Consequently, this process, and that of ocean crust generation, is not directly driven from below, but is a product of the tensional stresses that allow decompression and ascent of asthenospheric material, which reaches the mantle solidus in the uppermost 50 km or so.

Although we have been at pains to emphasize that many constructive margins may be passive, extensional features (Figure 2.10), nevertheless it is true that some thermal disturbances do occur in the upper mantle, where temperature variations may be as much as 200 °C (Figure 2.7). They are seen gravitationally, and, in the case of rising thermal plumes, may produce ocean island volcanoes. These occur because magma forms by partial melting in thermally anomalous upper mantle, and this magma penetrates the oceanic lithosphere. Hot-spot volcanism, such as occurs in the Hawaiian Islands, may result from such a thermal anomaly.

The purpose of this discussion has been to demonstrate that such thermal plumes are not a necessary feature of ridge volcanism. Indeed, many features of ocean ridges, such as their migration away from plates that are stationary in a hot-spot frame of reference (e.g. Africa, today — as described in Block 2), and their capacity to jump from one location to another, sometimes thousands of kilometres away, are more easily explained if they are passive features where two plates are separating rather than being located over zones of upwelling deep convection. In summary, **passive rifting** occurs in zones of extensional lithospheric stress, whereas **active rifting** occurs over deep thermal anomalies. The latter may be a necessary precursor for the formation, or initiation of an oceanic spreading ridge, as you will find in Block 2, whereas, once formed, ridges may propagate by passive rifting.

16

Summary

In Section 2.1.1, we have arrived at the following statements about the oceanic lithosphere:

1   The decrease in heat flow and increase in ocean depth with the square root of age holds good for oceanic lithosphere less than 60 Ma in age. The time constants governing the relationships between these parameters are satisfied by the cooling and contraction of a 125 km thick column of material.

2   The plate model for oceanic lithosphere requires a constant lithosphere thickness (*c.* 125 km) and basal isotherm (*c.* 1 350 °C); cooling of the lithosphere with age takes place from within. The boundary layer model requires a constant heat flow from the base of a thickening plate.

3   Both models accurately reflect the thermal structure of oceanic lithosphere produced by passive rifting due to extensional stress, generated from subduction zones, being applied across oceanic plates. Under these circumstances, new oceanic lithosphere may form by the adiabatic rise and partial melting of asthenosphere because of extensional decompression. This allows an almost horizontal 1 350 °C isotherm to be maintained at 100–125 km (Figure 2.10), while an extensive zone of shallow (0–50 km) partial melting occurs beneath the ridge, and isotherms at lower temperatures increase their depth with age to either side.

4   The boundary layer model provides the best description of the physical deformation behaviour of the oceanic lithosphere. An upper, rigid, heat conducting layer, the mechanical boundary layer of the Earth, is separated from the asthenosphere (which behaves plastically) by a viscous thermal boundary layer. This is coupled viscously to the rigid layer above yet is also capable of slow convection.

5   The optimum definition of the lithosphere–asthenosphere boundary is the depth of intersection between the steep thermal gradient of the conductive layer above and the shallow adiabatic thermal gradient of the convecting asthenosphere. Thermal modelling then predicts a typical increase in lithosphere thickness from zero at an erupting ocean ridge to 35 km after 5 Ma, to 60 km after 10 Ma, reaching a steady-state thickness of 125 km after 60 Ma. The steady state is thought to be maintained by convection in the asthenosphere.

6   While some ocean ridges may be associated with active rifting due to ascent of thermal plumes from the deeper mantle (Figure 2.7), this is not a necessary prerequisite for lithospheric extension, and most ocean ridges are thought to propagate by the kind of passive rifting (Figure 2.10) implicit in statements 3 and 4 above.

2.1.2 Continental lithosphere

There are various reasons why the continental lithosphere is poorly understood compared with the oceanic lithosphere. For example, its geological complexity, both vertically and horizontally, and the much longer time over which it has evolved are obvious factors. This Course is largely concerned with *processes* in the continental lithosphere; here we shall examine briefly some of the geophysical evidence that has led to a continuing debate between those who argue that continental lithosphere thickness need be no greater than that of normal oceans and others who believe that old continental lithosphere, in particular, may be as much as 300–400 km thick.

As you might expect, subcontinental temperatures are an important feature in the debate, and these are reflected in surface heat flow.

> But is continental heat flow simply a function of plate thickness, as in old ocean basins?

You may recall that there are very significant radiogenic heat sources within the continental lithosphere, and that these have become concentrated by geochemical processes into the upper crust. Heat is liberated by the decay of long-lived radioactive isotopes of which ^{238}U, ^{235}U, ^{232}Th and ^{40}K are the most important. Although their abundances can be measured from surface rocks, unfortunately the exact distribution of these isotopes, and therefore of heat production with depth in the lithosphere is poorly known, and estimates based on geological and petrological arguments are necessary. A major contribution to this subject, dating from the late 1960s and 1970s, was that continental heat flow could be assessed on a province by province basis. Within any one region with a uniform geological and tectonic history, surface heat flow (q) was found to correlate with radiogenic heat produced in surface rocks (A) by the linear equation:

$$q = bA + q^*\tag{2.3}$$

where b is the gradient of the line, and q^* is the intercept (the reduced heat flow).

An example of this relationship is illustrated in Figure 2.11a, which takes a single continental province, in this case the eastern USA, and plots surface heat flow against surface heat production for different parts of the province. Clearly, the greater the heat production in surface crustal rocks, the greater the heat flow and the relationship between the two is described by the gradient (b) in equation 2.3. There are various interpretations of the meaning of this gradient, and in the simplest model it is the thickness of the radioactive layer — 7.5 km in the case of Figure 2.11a. This interpretation is probably an oversimplification, and b is more commonly and successfully used to describe the way in which heat production falls off exponentially with increasing depth in the upper crust. The details need not concern us here, except to say that as this layer becomes progressively more eroded away so surface heat production also falls, together with surface heat flow.

Imagine what would happen in the hypothetical case that all the radioactive upper crustal layer were removed, so that there was negligible or zero surface heat production (i.e. $bA = 0$ in equation 2.3). The value of heat flow would be q^*, the intercept of our q–A correlation in Figure 2.11a with the heat flow axis. This quantity, q^*, is known as the **reduced heat flow** and it is commonly thought to represent the heat flowing from the lower crust and mantle. A plot of mean heat flow ($\bar{q}$) within each province that has been studied (i.e. the mean of all values in graphs such as Figure 2.11a for each province) against the reduced heat flow (q^*), shown in Figure 2.11b, also reveals a very approximate simple correlation.

ITQ 2.4 (a) Write down an equation representing the correlation between q^* and $\bar{q}$, the mean heat flow for continental heat flow provinces.

(b) What proportion of continental heat flow arises from radiogenic sources in the upper crust?

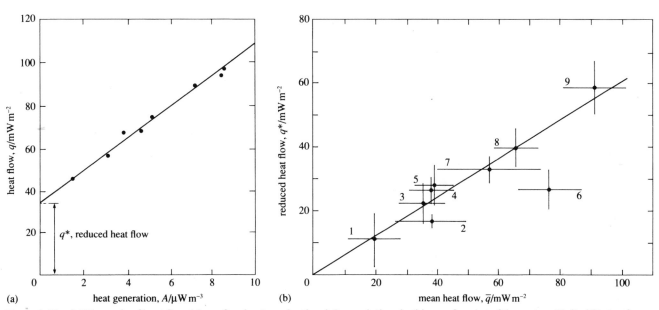

Figure 2.11 (a) Example of heat flow (q), surface heat production (A) correlation, in this case for part of the eastern United States, from which equation 2.3 was derived. (b) Plot of reduced heat flow (q^*) from the intercepts of q–A correlations as in (a) against mean heat flow ($\bar{q}$) for the following provinces: 1, Niger; 2, Baltic Shield; 3, Sierra Nevada; 4, western Australia; 5, Canadian Shield; 6, eastern United States; 7, Zambia; 8, central Australia; 9, Basin and Range Province, United States. (The value of q^* plotted for province 6 is lower than in (a) because several such correlations were taken into account.)

Thus we can eliminate one of the greatest uncertainties in continental heat flow studies, upper crustal radiogenic heat, and concentrate on $q*$ to estimate the thickness (z) of the conductive layer (i.e. the remainder of the lithosphere) beneath. We can do this because heat flow in a layer depends only on thermal conductivity (k) and temperature gradient ($\Delta T/z$):

$$q = k\frac{\Delta T}{z} \qquad (2.4)$$

We can estimate k (typically about 3 W m^{-1} K^{-1}) and also the likely temperature at the lithosphere–asthenosphere boundary, giving an estimate of ΔT, so that z can be calculated. For example, take a piece of continental lithosphere with a mean heat flow of 60 mW m^{-2}, an upper crustal thickness of 15 km and thermal conductivity 3 W m^{-1} K^{-1}. The reduced heat flow will be $60 \times 0.6 = 36$ mW m^{-2}. The temperature difference across the upper crust is calculated from equation 2.4 as:

$$\Delta T = \frac{qz}{k} = \frac{60 \times 10^{-3} \times 15 \times 10^{3}}{3.0} = 300\,°C$$

This will be a fair approximation to the temperature at 15 km depth where the heat flow is 36 mW m^{-2}. If we look for a temperature of 1 350 °C at the lithosphere–asthenosphere boundary (as in Section 2.1.1), ΔT across the rest of the lithosphere will be $1\,350 - 300 = 1\,050$ °C. Again, using equation 2.4, the thickness of this zone will be:

$$z = \frac{k\Delta T}{q*} = \frac{3.0 \times 1\,050}{36 \times 10^{-3}} = 87\,500 \text{ m, or } 87.5 \text{ km.}$$

The overall thickness of the lithosphere associated with a mean surface heat flow of 60 mW m^{-2} is therefore, very approximately, $87.5 + 15 = 102.5$ km. Although we have made several assumptions in arriving at this value, as you will see below, it is quite a good estimate of continental lithosphere thickness at this heat flow.

In refining calculations such as this, an allowance must usually be made for the small amounts of heat produced in the lower crust and mantle. As you know, a gradual reduction of radioactivity and, therefore, of conductive heat flow with depth from the surface must mean that the temperature gradient falls at the same rate. The thermal gradients in the example we have just calculated are $300/15 = 20$ °C km^{-1} in the upper crust and $1\,050/87.5 = 12$ °C km^{-1} across the rest of the lithosphere. So, unlike oceanic *conductive* geotherms (Figures 2.2, 2.6b and 2.9), geotherms in the continental lithosphere will be quite strongly *curved* (towards lower $\Delta T/z$ with greater z). The degree of curvature is governed (i) by the proportion of heat flow generated by upper crustal sources, as described above, and (ii) by the proportion of heat flow being conducted from deeper sources. The two are interrelated (Figure 2.11b and ITQ 2.4) so we can calculate a lithospheric geotherm for any continental region with a particular value of mean heat flow. Further examples are illustrated in Figure 2.12 together with the mantle adiabat and solidus curves that you have already encountered (e.g. Figure 2.9).

ITQ 2.5 (a) Using the intersections of the calculated geotherms with the mantle adiabat in Figure 2.12, complete Table 2.2 to provide a record of continental lithosphere thickness and basal temperatures for different values of surface heat flow. We have provided values for a 75 mW m^{-2} heat flow rather than putting another geotherm on Figure 2.12.

(b) The best estimate of the overall mean heat flow from the continents is 57 mW m^{-2}; that for regions younger than 250 Ma is 75 mW m^{-2} decreasing to a mean of 46 mW m^{-2} for regions older than 1 700 Ma. What does this imply about the thickness of the continental lithosphere beneath different crustal provinces?

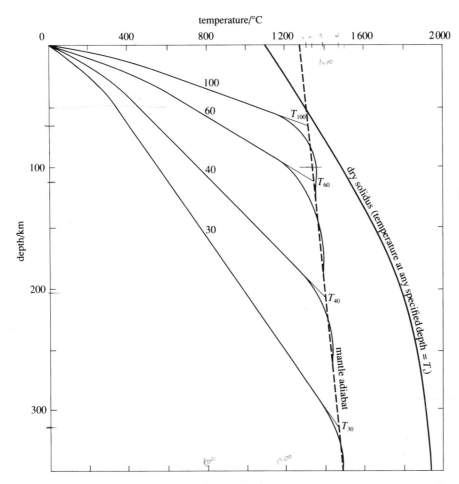

Figure 2.12 Estimated continental geotherms for different values of mean surface heat flow, ranging from 30 to 100 mW m^{-2}, intersections between extrapolated conductive upper mantle geotherms and the adiabat are labelled T with a subscript referring to the surface heat flow.

Table 2.2 Continental lithosphere thickness, basal temperatures and heat flow according to the models in Figure 2.12 (for use with ITQ 2.5)

Mean heat flow mW m^{-2}	Lithosphere thickness/km	Lithosphere basal temperature/°C
100	65	1300
75	100	1 340
60	110	1360
40	205	1400
30	315	1470

So the mean heat flow for continental areas leads to a lithosphere thickness of nearly 125 km. Surprisingly, this is exactly the same value as for normal oceans over 60 Ma old! But older continental areas appear to have a thicker lithosphere, a feature we need to examine in a little more detail. Going back to Figure 2.11b, you will see that four of the five provinces with mean heat flow less than 40 mW m^{-2} are the continental 'shield' or craton areas of Africa (Niger), the Baltic, Western Australia and Canada, all of which formed in the Archaean (> 2 500 Ma ago). According to Figure 2.12, the lithosphere beneath these regions exceeds 200 km thick and in Niger may exceed 300 km. Using this kind of analysis, in the late 1970s Henry Pollack and David Chapman of the University of Michigan studied the global distribution of heat flow and compiled a map of lithosphere thickness around the world, which we reproduce as Figure 2.13.

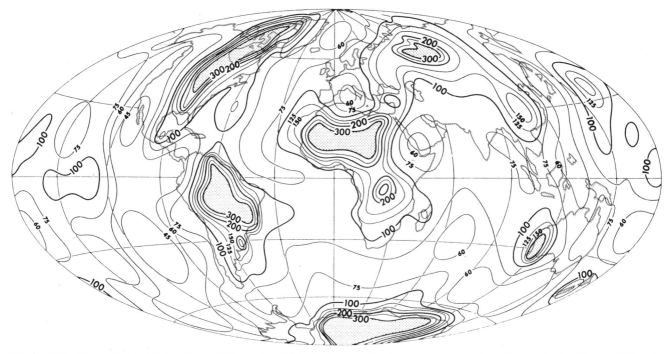

Figure 2.13 Map of global lithosphere thickness in which the intersection between computed geotherms (as in Figure 2.12) and temperatures that are 85% of the mantle solidus were used to estimate thickness. For reasons discussed in the text, this procedure may exaggerate the contrasts in lithosphere thickness.

The concept of a thermal boundary layer, which must exist beneath *both* oceans and continents — Figures 2.9 and 2.12 — had not been fully developed when Figure 2.13 was first produced. The approach adopted by Pollack and Chapman in both oceanic and continental areas was to determine the depth at which each lithospheric geotherm reached a temperature with a value 85% of the dry mantle solidus. It was argued that at this temperature, especially in the presence of small amounts of water, the lithosphere material would become less rigid in advance of melting and that such a temperature might, more reasonably than the depth at which the geotherm reached dry solidus itself, correspond to the lithosphere–asthenosphere boundary. The temperature of the dry solidus (T_s) at the surface is 1 100 °C, at 100 km depth it is 1 480 °C and at 200 km depth it is 1 780 °C, so the temperatures of 'softening' on the Pollack and Chapman model ($0.85T_s$) are 935 °C at the surface, 1 260 °C at 100 km depth and 1 510 °C at 200 km depth. You should use these values to sketch the form of the $0.85T_s$ curve on Figures 2.9 and 2.12.

> What effect would this approach to defining the lithosphere–asthenosphere boundary have on our estimates of lithosphere thickness for intersections in the shallow region (say, 60 km depth — refer to your 10 Ma geotherm in Figure 2.9) and in the deepest region (200–300 km depth — refer to Figure 2.12)?

The 10 Ma old oceanic geotherm reaches the $0.85T_s$ temperature (around 1 100 °C) at a *shallower* depth, just under 50 km instead of 60 km. In contrast, because of the widening temperature gap between the adiabat and the solidus at deep levels (Figure 2.12), conductive geotherms will reach $0.85T_s$ at *greater* depths than the adiabat (for example, a projection of the conductive part of the 40 mW m^{-2} geotherm in Figure 2.12 will reach the $0.85T_s$ curve at about 240 km rather than meeting the adiabat at 210 km.) Thus, although Figure 2.13 is extremely useful in depicting variations in lithosphere thickness, it tends to exaggerate them compared with the values that would be deduced from our modern definition of the lithosphere–asthenosphere boundary (i.e. the depth of intersection between conductive geotherms, as projected downwards, and the mantle adiabat). Remember that the adiabat describes the temperature profile of convecting material, able to deform plastically due to thermal processes in the mantle, whereas the solidus has more to do with partial melting and allows us to deduce where partial melt will occur.

In summary, in Figure 2.13, at depths shallower than 125 km (the depth at which the adiabat is actually at about $0.85T_s$) lithosphere thicknesses are underestimated, and at depths greater than 125 km they are overestimated. Nevertheless, it is very clear from Figure 2.13 that oceanic lithosphere, in general, is not quite as thick as continental lithosphere and that the lithosphere is particularly thick under continental shields (e.g. in Canada, Brazil, Antarctica, Africa, Siberia and W Australia). Notice, however, that continental lithosphere is thinner than average where heat flow is high in the western USA and NE Africa–Arabia, areas of special tectonic interest that we shall be discussing later.

These major lithospheric provinces are shown on the Tectonic Map of the Earth (TMOE), where the shields are shown as crustal provinces ranging in age from 1.6–2.5 Ga (PC_3), through 2.5–3.5 Ga (PC_2) to over 3.5 Ga (PC_1). The areas of thinner continental lithosphere in the western USA (the Basin and Range Province) and NE Africa–Arabia are generally younger Precambrian crust (e.g. PC_4 and PC_5) and are often associated with crustal rifting and separation (in the Red Sea–Afar region, for instance). The processes associated with such crustal rifting, separation and formation of oceanic lithosphere are described in Block 2.

Other recent analyses of heat flow and heat production in continental areas have further reduced the estimated thickness of the lithosphere. In particular, John Sclater's group, then at the Massachusetts Institute of Technology, showed in the early 1980s that continental heat sources due to magmatism and other tectonic disturbances, including frictional heating, may be more important than previously considered. The effect of these additional heat sources is rather complicated, but it is the resulting deduction that is important: *that their presence causes a reduction in estimated lithosphere thickness*. The argument goes like this — the heat from magmatism and friction is lost, or decays to negligible contributions, after 300–500 Ma. After this has happened, surface heat flow from the older continental lithosphere then depends on heat production and lithosphere thickness (because $\Delta T/z$ is proportional to q as explained earlier — equation 2.4). Sclater argues that, because additional heat sources are important in young lithosphere, the overall contribution of radiogenic heat production to heat flow must be less than previously estimated (i.e. less than the 40% we inferred from Figure 2.11b). So, given that we know the heat flow from older lithosphere, and given that this has less heat production than we first thought, to provide a greater contribution to surface heat flow from the base of the lithosphere, the lower parts of the geotherms in Figure 2.12 must be associated with a slightly higher thermal gradient. In other words, the geotherms are straightened slightly and intersect the mantle adiabat at slightly shallower depths (smaller z). The basal lithosphere contribution to surface heat flow is therefore increased, and the estimated thickness of the lithosphere is reduced.

You need not worry if you found this argument difficult to follow; you should note, however, that even this analysis indicates that the oldest and coldest parts of the lithosphere extend to about 200 km depth, in keeping with our deductions in ITQ 2.5. If you are now thinking that estimates of lithosphere thickness derived from heat flow are subject to great uncertainty, we agree! But despite the complications of inferring mantle geotherms from surface heat flow, this analysis is an important first step in understanding the behaviour of the lithosphere, which, in turn, depends on temperature as well as composition and other variables.

Fortunately, several other lines of evidence bear on the thickness of the continental lithosphere. First, xenoliths of mantle material are brought up with magmas and occur particularly in volcanic vents, such as **kimberlite pipes***; which are common in Archaean shields. (Such xenoliths occur in the Scottish Midland Valley where they are used, in Block 2, to evaluate the thickness of the Carboniferous lithosphere. In Block 5, xenolith samples are used to evaluate the mineralogy and composition of the lower crust). A range of these materials has been geochemically analysed with a view to determining their age and the pressure (P) and temperature (T) at which they

---

*Kimberlite pipes, named after the Kimberley area of South Africa, are volcanic vents formed by solid–gas volcanism; they contain fragments of garnet-rich peridotite, often with diamonds, all set in a fine-grained mica-rich matrix.

22

crystallized. The technique requires the analysis of minerals that equilibrate to produce slightly different chemical compositions at different P–T conditions — the principles will be discussed in Block 4. These samples yield depths up to 200 km and temperatures up to 1 400 °C (Figure 2.14). A particularly well-documented suite of 90 Ma old diamond-bearing kimberlites from the Kimberley area (S Africa) became part of the subcratonic lithosphere about 3 200 Ma ago and yield temperatures of 1 150 °C (well within the mechanical boundary layer) at a source depth of 180 km. Many of these data fall close to the 40 mW m^{-2} geotherm in Figure 2.12 and imply for this Archaean lithosphere a maximum continental lithosphere thickness close to 200 km.

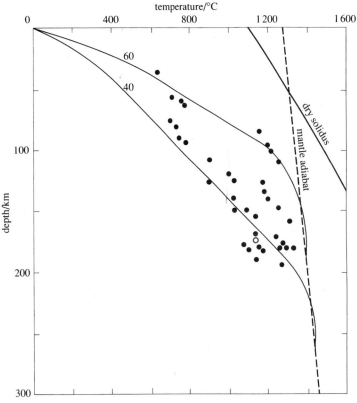

Figure 2.14   Comparison of the 40 and 60 mW m^{-2} geotherms from Figure 2.12 with P–T conditions derived from mineral compositions in a range of xenoliths from the sub-continental mantle. The ○ represents the well-documented 3 200 Ma old Kimberley material that came to the surface 90 Ma ago.

Another way of estimating lithosphere thickness arises from studies of the **thermal subsidence histories** produced by extension of intracontinental sedimentary basins, such as the North Sea. This is illustrated in videocassette VC 271 *Extensional Tectonics*, which you will need to watch at the end of Section 3.2. The essential features are summarized in Figure 2.15, where a section of lithosphere with original width x and thickness a is thinned simply by extension to final width $2x$ and thickness $0.5a$ (this is a **stretching factor**, given the symbol β, of 2 where β = initial thickness/final thickness). During the extensional phase, the upper crust cracks by brittle failure to form low-angle normal (extensional) faults which allow a graben to develop; the lower crust flows in a ductile fashion, and the lithosphere itself thins by plastic deformation (further details in Section 2.2). The overall effect is akin to that at ocean ridges (Figure 2.10), though not quite so dramatic in that the adiabatically rising asthenosphere may not reach a level, shallower than 50 km, where *extensive* partial melting is possible. If it did, then the process could lead to continental separation and the formation of a new spreading ocean (e.g. the Red Sea — discussed in Block 2). In some sedimentary basins, this process starts with the formation of basalt dykes and lava flows, but is then arrested if the stretching forces do not persist.

The important factor from our point of view is that the initial tectonic subsidence due to stretching (Figure 2.15b) is followed by **thermal subsidence** (Figure 2.15c) in which the isotherms associated with the dome of risen asthenosphere fall during cooling. In this way, the displaced hot asthenosphere cools back to lithosphere geotherm

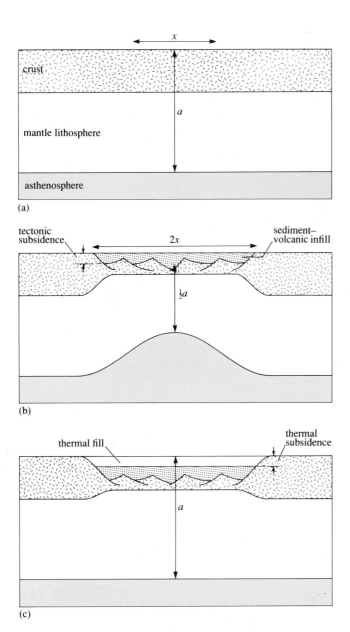

Figure 2.15 Simplified sequence of events following the formation of a sedimentary basin by lithospheric extension with a stretch factor (β) of 2, according to a model proposed by D. P. McKenzie of Cambridge University. Initial tectonic subsidence (b) is accompanied by the upwards convection of adiabatically rising asthenosphere to replace the attenuated lithosphere. This is followed (c) by gradual thermal subsidence as the risen asthenosphere cools back to the prevailing conductive geotherm. The time taken for the geotherm to return to its prestretching path is proportional to lithosphere thickness, so the thermal subsidence can be used to estimate a value for lithosphere thickness.

temperatures and becomes part of the lithosphere. The process is analogous to the cooling and thickening of oceanic lithosphere, except that the initial stages, where oceanic lithosphere reaches 60 km thickness in 10 Ma, are missing because the continental lithosphere in Figure 2.15b is already half the full thickness before cooling. However, like the depth of the ocean floor, the subsidence of basins on continental lithosphere almost follows a $t^{0.5}$ relationship (cf. equation 2.2). It follows that the greater the subsidence for a given amount of stretching, the thicker must be the lithosphere. Moreover, the thicker the lithosphere, the larger will be the value of K in equation 2.2 (see ITQ 2.1). A most impressive result is that the depth–time constant (K) derived from the subsidence of basins developed by extensional stresses in average continental lithosphere is virtually indistinguishable from that obtained for oceanic lithosphere subsidence (350 m Ma$^{-0.5}$, see ITQ 2.1).

What must this imply about the relative thickness of the contracting masses and thus about the thicknesses of oceanic and continental lithosphere at equilibrium?

A similar depth–time constant must require a similar lithospheric thickness and a similar basal temperature. Note that, as with oceanic lithosphere, the contracting column thickness is that of the plate model — the whole 125 km section, which, after 60 Ma, becomes the equilibrium thickness of what we have defined as the lithospheric plate on the boundary layer model. A greater equilibrium thickness would apply for old continental lithosphere > 250 Ma old, with lower than the mean heat flow value. Most sedimentary basins that have been studied in this way are of Mesozoic and Cenozoic age, developed on mainly late Precambrian and younger lithosphere, which would have average values of heat flow ($c.$ 60 mW m^{-2}). *So the results of thermal subsidence confirm our earlier deduction from heat flow that typical continental lithosphere is 100–125 km thick, the same as oceanic lithosphere.*

A final approach to the problem of continental lithosphere thickness derives from *seismic data.* Of course, seismic wave transmission depends on the elastic moduli and density of the media through which they travel. Both elastic moduli and density increase with pressure, hence depth, and temperature inside the Earth, but elastic moduli increase more rapidly than density.

> There is a particular zone within the upper mantle (i.e. the top 400 km) where there is a deviation from otherwise uniform elasticity over the short time-scales required for the passage of seismic waves. Can you recall what this zone is called and what is thought to be happening here to the material of the upper mantle?

This is the *low velocity zone,* where both P-wave and S-wave speeds are reduced by up to 10%; the cause is thought to be the presence of a small percentage of partial melt within otherwise solid peridotite. Not only is their speed reduced, but the seismic waves are reduced in amplitude due to energy loss; the latter effect is known as **seismic wave attenuation**. You should not be surprised to learn that the zone is found to be most prominent at depths of 5–30 km beneath ocean ridges (cf. Figure 2.10), but is also present between 100 and 200 km depth elsewhere in oceanic areas. At these depths (Figure 2.9), the geotherm makes its closest approach to the dry solidus. As we noted earlier, the presence of small amounts of water and other volatiles will reduce the melting temperature, so it is not surprising that there is limited partial melting in much of the asthenosphere beneath the oceans. You should note that while there will be an asthenosphere at some depth everywhere, this does not necessarily imply that there must be a low velocity zone. This is because the asthenosphere occurs wherever temperatures approach the mantle adiabat, which, at deep levels, is at lower temperatures than the dry, or even the wet, solidus that is required for partial melting (further details in Block 2).

At one time, the base of the lithosphere was defined as being coincident with the top of the low velocity zone, itself the top of the asthenosphere. But, as you will now appreciate, the lithosphere–asthenosphere boundary is related to long-term plastic deformation, whereas the low velocity zone is defined on short-term elastic criteria. Moreover, the low velocity zone is absent beneath many continental areas. It does occur at 100–150 km depth beneath most young areas, again where the geotherm and solidus are close (Figure 2.12) but is difficult to locate elsewhere. However, during the early to mid-1980s, a detailed study of P-wave transmissions through the mantle beneath the Proterozoic shield of northern Australia identified a low velocity zone between 200 and 325 km depth, and this has now been confirmed elsewhere, as you will find shortly.

Similarly, studies of *shear waves,* in the range 10°–60° epicentral angles (i.e. surface distances of 1 100 to 6 600 km) have been used in several continents to identify differences between the mantle lithosphere beneath shields and younger tectonic areas. A particular part of the seismic wave trace known as the **SS phase** has been particularly useful: this is a kind of 'double' S-wave that has undergone one reflection at the surface to produce a secondary S-wave, which follows a similar path to the first (Figure 2.16a). The wave form of arrivals is distinctive, comprising three distinct sets of arrivals. Observations across a range of epicentral angles can be used to construct velocity–depth profiles based on the time of arrivals for each distance as shown in Figure 2.16b. An obvious drawback is that the deeper parts of the velocity–

depth profile require longer travel paths, so that the deeper seismic waves are sampling a larger volume of mantle. The picture presented in Figure 2.16b therefore required the analysis of data from many stations and is an average picture for (i) TNA (Tectonic North America), which is the tectonically active area of Western North America and the Eastern Pacific, and (ii) SNA (Shield North America), where wave transmission was almost entirely within the Canadian Shield. Figure 2.16b extends down to 900 km, well into the mantle *transition zone,* where there is a rapid increase in wave velocity due to the increases in elastic moduli and density associated with phase changes. Olivine, the principal upper mantle mineral, changes under pressure to new, more compact mineral structures in a series of steps at different depths.

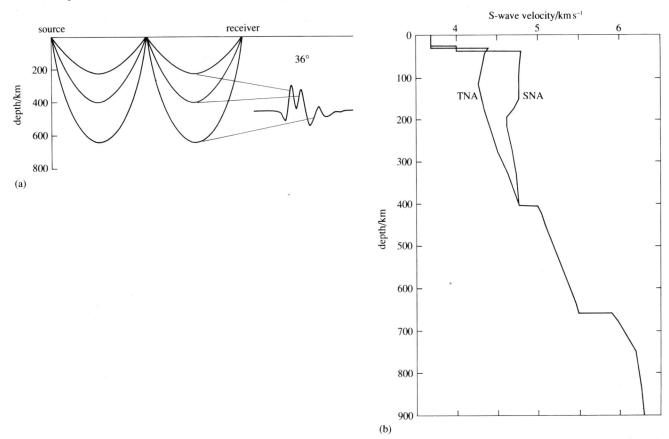

Figure 2.16 (a) Schematic illustration showing the composition of an SS seismic wave at an epicentral angle of 36°. The wave shape is distinctive, comprising three arrivals, but varies in detail with distance from the source. (b) S-wave velocity–depth profiles deduced from SS arrivals for tectonically active (TNA) and Precambrian shield (SNA) areas in North America.

> **ITQ 2.6** (a) Look carefully at Figure 2.16b; identify the depths of the crust–mantle boundary (the Moho) and the top of the mantle transition zone.
>
> (b) Describe the differences between the two velocity profiles. Would you say that both contain a low velocity zone? At what depth is the minimum upper mantle S-wave velocity recorded?

So seismic SS phase analysis identifies a clear difference between the upper mantle shear wave velocity structure beneath shields and tectonically active areas. But what does all this seismic information tell us about upper mantle conditions and the thickness of the lithosphere? First, the depth of the low velocity zone in the TNA profile of Figure 2.16b (*c.* 110–120 km) actually corresponds closely with the uppermost parts of the asthenosphere as proposed from thermal modelling, along high heat flow geotherms; and this suggests that the uppermost parts of the asthenosphere in this tectonically active area are actually partially molten. Given that surface heat flow will lie between 75 and 100 mW m^{-2} (ITQ 2.5), reference to Figure 2.12 shows that the lithosphere should be between 70 and 100 km thick (see also Table 2.2). Also from Figure 2.12, geotherm temperatures at these depths make their closest approach to the dry solidus. So the presence of a low velocity zone centred on 110–120 km depth again suggests that water and/or other volatiles are available in this part of the mantle to reduce the melting temperature (further details in Block 2). Note, however, that as lithosphere thickness increases, so temperatures at the top of the deeper asthenosphere are further from the solidus. So the possibility of partial melting even in the presence of volatiles is reduced. This is borne out by the SNA profile (Figure 2.16), which indicates a thicker lithosphere, around 200 km deep. Again this is consistent with the results of thermal modelling on geotherms with lower surface heat flow (Figure 2.12) and with mantle xenolith studies from shield areas (e.g. the African shield data in Figure 2.14). Rather than reflecting the presence of partial melt, the lower velocity portion of the SNA profile at *c*. 200 km depth is probably due to a strong seismic contrast between warm asthenosphere close to adiabatic temperatures and the cold, rigid, high velocity plate above.

The overall difference in propagation velocity between shield and tectonic areas must, at least partly, reflect their contrasting thermal structures, with the shield, on average, being much colder, less elastic and having the higher shear wave velocity. But notice from Figure 2.16b that the two seismic profiles are not coincident until they reach 400 km depth (though it has to be said that the resolution of the data from such deep profiles is rather poor). Surely, on thermal arguments, their temperatures should be identical and on the mantle adiabat from 200 to 400 km depth, where both areas have an asthenosphere? If not, does this mean that the asthenospheric mantle beneath the shield is cooler, therefore more dense, and thus perhaps a zone of large-scale mantle convective down-welling? Such flows would have obvious effects on the Earth's gravity field — there should be large-scale positive gravity anomalies — which are not observed. Remember that as with all seismic waves, shear wave velocities reflect both the elastic properties and density of the media through which they travel.

> Does this give any further clues to the possible reasons for seismic contrasts between tectonic and shield areas?

If the density is not significantly different, perhaps the elastic moduli are greater beneath shield areas than beneath tectonically active areas. One reason for this might be that the chemical composition is different with less compressible, more rigid material (i.e. larger values of elastic moduli) beneath the shields. As a rough guide, if the composition of olivine changes from Fo_{88} to Fo_{90}, to become slightly more magnesium rich, then the shear wave velocity increases by about 1%. Similarly, mantle peridotite from which about 5% of melt has been extracted also has a 1% increased shear wave velocity compared with similar 'undepleted' material from which no melt has been extracted. This all adds up to the inescapable and quite logical conclusion that the mantle beneath continental shields is chemically depleted, because of previous melting processes, and therefore is relatively **refractory** (i.e. difficult to melt) and less elastic than the mantle beneath active tectonic and oceanic areas. In view of the long period over which the continents have grown at the expense of the mantle beneath, it is not altogether surprising that the mantle lithosphere attached to continental shields is depleted and refractory. In terms of modern plate-tectonic analogies (Figure 2.17), the mantle beneath an active continental margin/island arc becomes chemically depleted by the melting processes that create continental crust; the mantle lithosphere and continental crust above may stay together, related by this common tectonic history, throughout the entire subsequent evolution of the lithosphere.

From the seismic differences between subcontinental 'shield' and 'tectonic' mantle, it seems likely that chemical differences may persist down to 400 km, in which case part of the asthenosphere would also be related physically and chemically to the continents. Could it be that the whole of the upper mantle (down to 400 km) associated with shield areas and not just the lithospheric plates has been moving as a coherent unit for hundreds or even thousands of millions of years (i.e. the time-scale for continental evolution)? The hypothesis that the 200–400 km deep asthenosphere beneath shield areas may well be both chemically depleted and cooler than elsewhere, and that it may stay attached to the mobile continents, led Thomas Jordan of Princeton University to propose the term **tectosphere**. This embraces the crust and a thick mantle layer, down to as much as 400 km depth, which are chemically and physically related through their common tectonic histories — hence the term 'tecto'-sphere. This concept allows the term lithosphere to be retained for the outermost layer of the Earth with significant strength, while the tectosphere embraces the deep roots of continental plates. If this model is right, then several other useful deductions follow: for example, (i) mantle convection cannot be confined to the upper 400 km, (ii) the upper mantle is unlikely to be chemically homogeneous, and (iii) there are likely to be lateral thermal gradients associated with deep continental structures. Indeed it may be that unlike oceanic lithosphere, which is recycled at subduction zones (Figure 2.17), the deep continental tectosphere roots are stabilized against convective disruption by the differences in composition due to past melting processes.

Summary

In Section 2.1.2, we have examined the evidence for the thermal structure and thickness of the continental lithosphere, and have made the following observations and deductions:

1 Radioactive isotopes enriched in the upper crust cause a higher thermal gradient to be established than in the deeper, less radiothermal parts of the continental lithosphere, so continental geotherms are more curved than those of oceanic lithosphere. Analysis of heat flow–heat production relationships from continental heat flow provinces (Figure 2.11, equation 2.3) shows that roughly 40% of continental heat flow arises from these shallow radiothermal sources, though recent work suggests this may be an overestimate, because the effects of magmatic and frictional heating in young continental provinces were previously underestimated.

2 Using calculated geotherms (Figure 2.12) and the same definition of the lithosphere–asthenosphere boundary as for oceanic areas (i.e. treating the continental lithosphere as a boundary layer), the continental lithosphere varies from $c.$ 70–100 km thick when mean heat flow is 75–100 mW m^{-2} in young and tectonically active crustal provinces, increasing to 110–125 km thick at average continental heat flows of $c.$ 60 mW m^{-2}, and to between 200 and 300 km thick when heat flow is 30–40 mW m^{-2} in ancient Precambrian shield areas. (Note there are very few provinces with a mean heat flow much lower than 40 mW m^{-2}, so there is probably very little lithosphere thicker than 200 km.) A most remarkable result is that the mean heat flow for continental areas leads to a lithosphere thickness of almost 125 km, the same value as for oceanic lithosphere over 60 Ma old.

3 Estimates of equilibration pressures and temperatures based on the chemistry of mineral phases from diamond-bearing kimberlite pipes produce values falling close to the calculated 40 mW m^{-2} geotherm (Figure 2.14) thus reaffirming an estimated lithosphere thickness of $c.$ 180–200 km for a 3 200 Ma shield area in South Africa.

4 The thermal subsidence histories of sedimentary basins developed on typical continental lithosphere, with heat flow close to the mean (Figure 2.15), produce a thermal depth–time constant (equation 2.2) virtually indistinguishable from that obtained from subsidence of the oceanic lithosphere. Modelling of these results confirms that average continental lithosphere is 100–125 km thick. Subsidence is due to the cooling and contraction of upwardly displaced, hot (adiabatic) asthenosphere, which rises when the lithosphere is stretched and thinned; if stretching forces persist, continental separation will occur.

5 At particular depths in the upper mantle, velocity–depth profiles show a seismic low velocity zone, well illustrated by the seismic wave SS phase. Beneath tectonically active areas (Figure 2.16), the low-velocity zone occurs at $c.$ 110–120 km depth, thus corresponding with the uppermost parts of the asthenosphere (top at 70–100 km) as deduced from thermal modelling. Here partial melting occurs, due to the close approach of calculated geotherms and the dry mantle solidus (Figure 2.12); some volatiles may be present, lowering the melting temperatures. SS phase data confirm the 200 km lithosphere thickness beneath shield areas; a newly recognized low velocity zone immediately beneath this depth is most probably due to the seismic contrast between hot, convecting asthenosphere material below and the cold rigid plate above. Thus deep low velocity zones are not necessarily due to partial melting.

6 The seismic and thermal contrasts between young and ancient shield-like continental lithosphere suggest that chemical differences between the two may persist to 400 km depth, partly as a result of past mantle depletion events leading to crust

formation above. Thus continental shields may remain physically attached to their own piece of asthenospheric mantle; the entire 400 km deep section is called the tectosphere. Chemical heterogeneities may therefore be present throughout the entire depth of the subcontinental mantle, and you will meet further evidence for this deduction as the Course develops.

Finally, Figure 2.17 summarizes some of the more important concepts we have discussed in Section 2.1; the next stage is to examine the mechanical behaviour of the lithosphere in more detail, including the influence of composition on that behaviour.

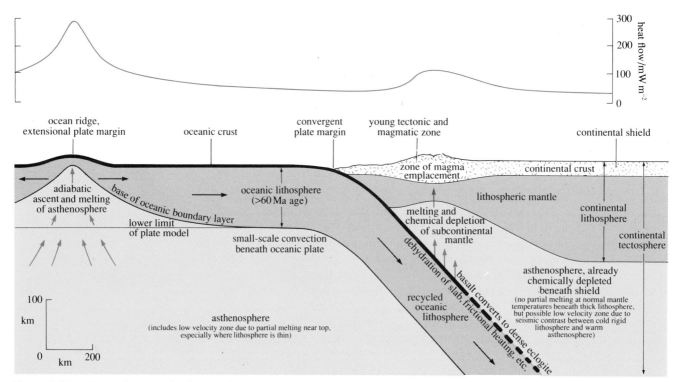

Figure 2.17 Approximate scale diagram for oceanic and continental crust and upper mantle showing the main features of the lithosphere and asthenosphere associated with modern extensional and ocean-continent convergent boundaries. The graph above the section gives probable values of heat flow.

2.2 LITHOSPHERE STRENGTH AND RHEOLOGY

The study of seismic wave transmission provides information on the short-term (0.1 s to 1 hour) mechanical behaviour of the lithosphere. On such a short time-scale, the material of the entire Earth behaves elastically and has sufficient rigidity to transmit seismic waves, except in the case of S-waves in partially molten zones. In particular, on this time-scale, the lithosphere behaves as a strong elastic and rigid body which has high values of elastic moduli. For example, a high compressibility modulus means that the lithosphere is relatively difficult to compress; it is incompressible compared with the lower velocity asthenosphere. Remember that elastic behaviour merely requires that a deformed body returns to its original shape after the stress is removed.

Naturally, however, this short-term, or **instantaneous strength** greatly exceeds the long-term strength of the same materials when subject to forces for tens or hundreds of millions of years. It is here that the concept of **dynamic viscosity** (η — the Greek letter eta) is useful as a means of defining strength, because it is the ability of a medium to resist motion due to shear stress. To remind you about this concept, consider Figure 2.18, where there is a fluid trapped between two blocks, the lower one fixed and the upper one moving. Because the fluid resists the motion of the upper block, a force F must be applied to sustain the motion in what we may call the x-direction (i.e. horizontally to the right). If we regard the fluid as being made up from a series of narrow layers, there will be a uniform change of velocity in the x-direction as we move down through the fluid in the y-direction (vertically). The velocity gradient can be defined as $\Delta v_x/\Delta y$ (Figure 2.18) and must be directly proportional to the applied force, F, and inversely proportional to the area of the blocks, A, so that:

$$\frac{\Delta v_x}{\Delta y} \propto \frac{F}{A} (= P)$$

where P, the *pressure* or *stress* is defined as force (newtons) per unit area (metres squared) and is expressed in pascals ($1\,Pa = 1\,N\,m^{-2}$). The constant of proportionality is the dynamic viscosity (η), which expresses the resistance of the fluid to shearing stress:

$$\frac{\eta \Delta v_x}{\Delta y} = P, \quad \text{hence } \eta = \frac{P\Delta y}{\Delta v_x} \qquad (2.5)$$

From equation 2.5, what will be the units of dynamic viscosity?

They will be the units of pressure, Pa, multiplied by distance, m, and divided by velocity, $m\,s^{-1}$: $Pa\,m/(m\,s^{-1})$, or Pa s. In essence then, dynamic viscosity is stress multiplied by time, and this implies that the longer it takes to transmit a particular stress, the more viscous will be the medium. Of course, even the most deformable materials must have some value of viscosity, and while that for the asthenosphere is *c.* 10^{20}–10^{21} Pa s, a typical value for the lower lithosphere would be 10^{22} Pa s, ranging up to 10^{25} Pa s in parts of the crust and upper mantle, sometimes down to *c.* 60 km depth. (For comparison, water has a dynamic viscosity of 10^{-3} Pa s, and that of molten basalt at the Earth's surface is 2.7×10^2 Pa s). These values have been determined by modelling the recovery behaviour of the Earth's surface in regions of isostatic change, such as following the melting of ice caps; this subject is reviewed in the second level Earth Science courses.

What does this imply about the relative strength and resistance to shear deformation of the asthenosphere, lower lithosphere and upper lithosphere?

Quite simply, in terms of their ability to resist long-term stresses, the asthenosphere is weaker and more easily deformed than the lower lithosphere, whereas the strongest, most rigid, and least deformable material seems to occur in the crust and upper mantle, that is the upper lithosphere. The dynamic viscosity of the lithosphere, which describes its strength when subject to shear deformation, is therefore a primary variable influencing the deformation behaviour, or **rheology** of the lithosphere. (Note that rheology is literally the science of deformation, whereas dynamic viscosity and strength are literally to do with the resistance of a material to an applied stress.)

What other *physical* variables might influence the rheology of the lithosphere?

The deformation behaviour must depend on the *magnitude of the applied stress*; the greater the stress, the more a given material will deform. *Temperature*, itself related to *heat flow* through the lithosphere (Figure 2.12), will also be important for its effect on strength, viscosity and hence rheology. For example, one idea we introduced in Section 2.1.2 was that mantle material starts to deform easily at $0.85 T_s$. Finally, as implied earlier, the *time* over which a given stress is applied must be critical, for the entire lithosphere and asthenosphere behave elastically and do not deform permanently when subject to short-term stresses (Figure 2.19a and b).

What types of deformation behaviour due to long-term stresses do we expect in the lithosphere? Well, in the uppermost zones, those accessible to geological observation, rocks are easily broken and fractured (e.g. jointing and faulting), representing **brittle deformation**, and this type of response extends to considerable depth in the crust. At the other end of the scale, the high temperature parts of the deep lithosphere with lower viscosity material may yield or flow under long-term stress. On an atomic scale, long-term shearing stresses are capable of exceeding the yield strength of solids and produce **inelastic (plastic) deformation** (Figure 2.19c) in which atomic dislocations, or even smaller adjustments due to crystal imperfections are exploited. On a larger scale, the solid appears to flow rather than fracture, so deformation in the deep lithosphere is known as **ductile flow** (ductile literally means

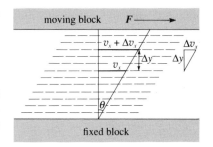

Figure 2.18 Deformation of a fluid under a shearing force (F) considered as sliding of adjacent layers parallel to a fixed block below and a moving block above. θ is the angle of shear and the velocity gradient is $\Delta v_x/\Delta y$.

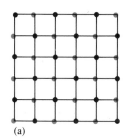

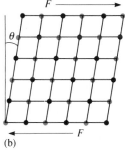

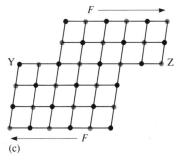

Figure 2.19 Shear deformation of an ionic crystal lattice within which atomic dislocations (as in c) occur, resulting in permanent, or inelastic deformation. (a) shows the original undeformed lattice, and (b) illustrates elastic deformation from which the crystal would recover the original shape if the stress (F) is removed. Once the angle of shear (θ) is increased beyond (b), due to a greater stress magnitude or time, the crystal deforms permanently by slip along the plane YZ.

'yielding'). Brittle and ductile deformation represent the two principal ways in which lithosphere material may be deformed permanently, both by *inelastic* processes.

To recap, brittle deformation will occur near the surface and ductile flow will occur in the deep, hotter parts of the lithosphere subject to long-term stresses. But what about the region between; do the brittle and ductile regions meet at some particular depth? We have good evidence from theoretical and modelling studies that lithosphere subject to small stresses (i.e. in tectonically stable areas of whatever age) has an intermediate elastic region separating the brittle and ductile zones. The presence of an undeformed mid-lithosphere region in some areas is supported by the results of seismic reflection profiling (see Block 1B). The vertical profile of deformation behaviour in such lithosphere is represented by a column taken through the left-hand side of Figure 2.20 (i.e. brittle–elastic–ductile with increasing depth). The asthenosphere, of course, will be even more ductile than the lowermost lithosphere because of its lower dynamic viscosity. The presence of an elastic zone within the lithosphere means that the lithosphere *as a whole* is still capable of resisting permanent deformation. So, if stresses are low and/or operate for a short enough time, a seismically elastic lithosphere can be envisaged as incorporating both viscously deformable and elastic zones. Materials that display both properties when subject to different magnitudes and durations of stress are known as viscoelastic, hence the concept that the Earth has a **viscoelastic lithosphere**.

What do you think will happen to the elastic layer if either the magnitude of the stress is increased or the time over which a particular stress operates increases?

Figure 2.20 illustrates the fate of the elastic layer, which gradually shrinks as the lithosphere is no longer able to resist the shearing stress. The regions of brittle and ductile deformation will extend downwards and upwards respectively until the elastic layer is reduced to zero (at point WLF, about half-way across Figure 2.20).

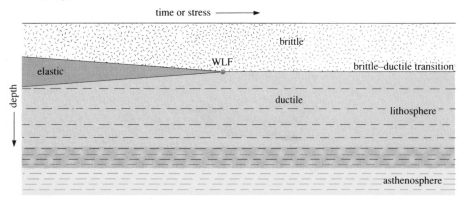

Figure 2.20 The relationship between brittle, elastic and ductile (viscoelastic, decreasing viscosity with depth) layers in tectonically stable areas (left) and in lithosphere subject to shearing or laterally directed stresses (right) of increasing magnitude or time. Note that the elastic layer disappears at WLF, which represents the point at which the *whole lithosphere* can *fail*, being unable to resist further stress without deforming permanently.

Another way of looking at this is to imagine an equal and uniform horizontal force operating on the entire lithosphere (Figure 2.21). The brittle layer fractures, particularly near the surface, but with increasing depth it progressively resists deformation because of viscous coupling to the elastic layer below. Therefore stress accumulates progressively with depth and reaches a maximum across the elastic layer (vertical part of solid curve), which resists permanent deformation. Beneath the elastic layer, there is progressively more ductile behaviour with depth, so the **accumulated stress** falls, reaching zero at the point where the amount of ductile flow has exactly compensated for the previously applied stress. As the horizontal force is maintained, so the accumulated stress on the elastic layer grows until, ultimately, the strength of the elastic layer will be exceeded resulting in the broken line. It is this stage that we have reached in the centre of Figure 2.20 where, past the point labelled WLF, no part of the lithosphere can resist permanent deformation so that **whole lithosphere failure (WLF)** occurs. The accumulated stress is released (i.e. the peak in Figure 2.21 now shrinks) by deformation and physical decoupling within the lithosphere, a process

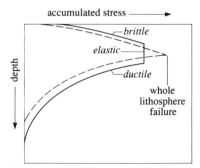

Figure 2.21 Schematic representation of stress accumulation across an elastic layer (solid line) when zones above and below are yielding by brittle and ductile deformation respectively. As in Figure 2.20, with increase in time or stress magnitude the regions of brittle and ductile deformation coalesce (dashed line) as the previously elastic layer starts to fail. After failure, stress is dissipated and so the peak diminishes as deformation proceeds.

we examine in more detail in Blocks 4–6. If the force is still maintained, as we approach the right of Figure 2.20, ultimately there is no accumulated stress in the lithosphere, which continues to deform in direct response to the applied stress. Note that another important variable in Figure 2.20 is temperature; the higher the lithosphere temperature, the more rapidly a given lithosphere column will reach failure: we shall look at this again later in this Section.

2.2.1 The effect of mineral strain rates

So far we have talked about the effects of *stress* on the lithosphere and you can see in Figure 2.21 how stress may be concentrated at a certain depth. But what about *strain* in the rocks?

What is the relationship between stress and strain?

Strain is the change brought about by a particular stress; it may be elastic or inelastic, but in what follows we shall be considering permanent, inelastic strain due to ductile flow. Strain is a way of measuring the amount of deformation that has occurred. For example, in the case of a horizontal stress the strain is the change in length (l) of a specified original length (L) of material: l/L (and is therefore dimensionless, being a ratio of two lengths). Since tectonic forces tend to be uniform over long periods of time with the result that strain is also uniform, a more useful property of geological materials is the **strain rate** l/Lt, which tells us by how much a particular material will deform in a given time. It is a ratio of two lengths divided by time and so has units of s^{-1}:

$$S\text{ (strain rate)} = \frac{l}{Lt} \quad [s^{-1}] \tag{2.6}$$

For example, what would be the total amount of strain after 10 Ma (i.e. after 3.13×10^{14} seconds) in a 1 m length of a material undergoing ductile deformation and with a uniform strain rate of $10^{-15}\,s^{-1}$?

A strain rate of $10^{-15}\,s^{-1}$ tells us that a 1 m length of material (in the simple case of horizontal stress) will change by $1 \times 10^{-15}\,m$ in one second. Thus in 10 Ma, or $3.13 \times 10^{14}\,s$, the length will have changed by 0.313 m, or by just over 30%. (Another way of looking at this is to say that from equation 2.6, $l = SLt = 10^{-15} \times 1 \times 3.13 \times 10^{14} = 0.313\,m$). Whether this is expansion or contraction will depend on the nature of the force, but notice that if all 30% of the strain deformation has occurred after 10 Ma, all the stress will have been dissipated. On a stress–depth profile such as Figure 2.21, the material would plot with zero accumulated stress.

To understand why strain rate is such a useful property of geological materials, you will need to study Figure 2.22. You will not be surprised to find that strain rates are extremely sensitive to temperature; here are plotted experimentally determined curves for a number of common minerals at a constant *extensional* stress of $50 \times 10^6\,Pa$ (50 MPa — megapascals — or 500 atmospheres, since 1 atm $\approx 10^5$ N m^{-2}, or Pa). Most active geological and tectonic processes take place at strain rates around 10^{-15} to $10^{-16}\,s^{-1}$ (e.g. spreading and subduction rates of 1–3 cm a^{-1} require 3–$9 \times 10^{-16}\,s^{-1}$ strain across 1 000 km lithosphere sections) though just a few are a great deal faster. Lower strain rates, $10^{-17}\,s^{-1}$ and smaller, are not geologically meaningful on the time-scales available. Note that a strain rate of $10^{-16}\,s^{-1}$ is a useful definition of the beginning of ductile flow in rocks (further discussion below).

> **ITQ 2.7** (a) Under extensional stress of 50 MPa, at what temperatures do quartz (wet and dry), plagioclase feldspar, pyroxene and olivine reach a geologically useful strain rate of $10^{-16}\,s^{-1}$ (note that temperatures must be higher for faster strain rates)?
>
> (b) Given that the mineralogy of the upper continental crust is dominated by quartz and feldspar, whereas that of the upper mantle is dominated by olivine, at what depths might you expect stress dissipation (ductile deformation) to start in these two layers along the 60 mW m^{-2} (average continental heat flow) geotherm in Figure 2.12?

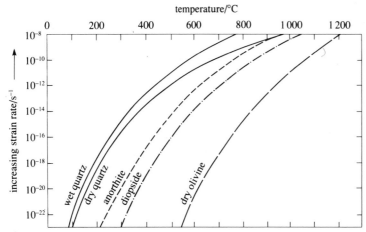

Figure 2.22 Experimentally determined variations in strain rate with temperature for several common minerals under an extensional stress of 50 MPa. The curve for wet quartz is included because small amounts of water present in the crust will make this more appropriate than the equivalent dry curve in some instances. (Under compressional stresses, rocks and minerals are much stronger, so these curves will be shifted to the right under compression at 50 MPa — this is discussed later in the text.)

We hope you will have spent some time studying Figure 2.22, and have compared your answer to ITQ 2.7 with ours. So far, we have avoided the layer between the upper crust and mantle — the lower crust — because we have no reliable and ubiquitous composition. However, it is often thought to comprise granulite (a metamorphic rock containing Ca-feldspar and Ca, Mg pyroxene represented by diopside) which would start to deform at 425 °C. This temperature is achieved on the 60 mW m^{-2} geotherm at only 25 km depth, so assuming the presence of anorthite, *it is highly likely that much of the lower crust will be ductile*. This subject of lower crustal compositions and their effect on rheology is discussed more fully in Block 5.

In summary, for a 60 mW m^{-2} geotherm and 50 MPa extensional stress, quartz-rich crystalline materials in the upper crust may become ductile below about 13 km; lower crustal feldspar-rich rocks will be ductile below about 25 km, and mantle olivine-rich rocks (peridotite) will become ductile at about 50 km depth. (Note that there is insufficient pyroxene in most peridotites for this mineral to affect mantle rheology significantly). Remember that these deductions are based on strain rates of 10^{-16} s^{-1} having been attained. In colder lithosphere, strain rates are slower and the material will not respond in a geologically meaningful time to the same applied stress; moreover, if the stress is less than 50 MPa, then all the curves in Figure 2.22 will move to the right, requiring higher temperatures to promote ductile behaviour. In fact, 50 MPa is probably rather high for the overall laterally directed lithospheric stress as we shall see in Section 2.2.2. Where strain rates of 10^{-16} s^{-1} are not attained, on geological time-scales we would think of the material as elastic, and while there may be a thin brittle layer in the uppermost crust, the majority of the lithosphere will remain undeformed. For example, at 50 MPa along the 40 mW m^{-2} geotherm (Figure 2.12), no crustal material would reach the temperatures required for ductile deformation, and even olivine-rich rocks will not become ductile until 100 km depth.

The rheological behaviour of compositionally layered continental lithosphere of the type you started to consider in ITQ 2.7 has been modelled in more detail by Nick Kusznir and Graham Park of Liverpool and Keele Universities. They started with a continental lithosphere divided into the same three layers (see right of Figure 2.23a) and with the same 60 mW m^{-2} heat flow geotherm that you considered in ITQ 2.7 and above. They then examined the effect of time on rheology by applying a continuous extensional force of 10^{12} N m^{-1} (force per unit length) along a section of the lithosphere. In a 100 km thick lithosphere, this is equivalent to a stress of 10^7 N m^{-2}, or 10 MPa. Figure 2.23a, based on the same principles as Figure 2.21, illustrates the sequence of deformation events as the 10 MPa stress is maintained for 1 Ma. At first, after 1 000 years in this low stress regime, there will be some depth in the mantle at which olivine is hot enough to become ductile — in fact at about 45 km depth. (So even with a stress of only 10 MPa, olivine becomes ductile on the Kusznir and Park model at only 45 km depth, close to the depth that we deduced in ITQ 2.7 for a

50 MPa stress; this may reflect a small difference between their mantle geotherms and ours in Figure 2.12, a difference that need not worry us here.) Above the 50 km level, no permanent deformation occurs within 1 000 years, and so the stress here is increased.

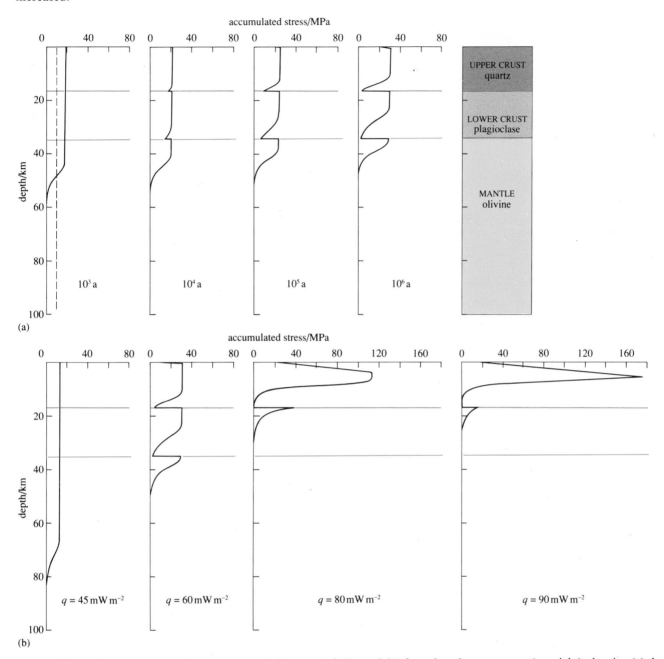

Figure 2.23 Lithosphere accumulated stress–depth diagrams (cf. Figure 2.21) for a three-layer structure (top right), showing (a) the effect of increasing time on rheological development at constant geothermal gradient (in this case that associated with a 60 mW m^{-2} heat flow), and (b) the effect of changing geothermal gradient at constant time (1 Ma). In all cases, a continuous extensional force of 10 MPa (10^{12} N m^{-1} along a lithospheric section of 100 km thickness) has been assumed.

Can you see why the stress above about 50 km depth has approached 20 MPa when the lithosphere itself is subject to a stress of 10 MPa?

This is because ductile flow has taken place in the lower lithosphere and so has dissipated stress there, so focusing the entire stress that *was* operating across a 100 km section (vertical line in Figure 2.23a for 10^3 years) onto the undeformed upper 50 km. As time progresses, stress continues to increase within the top 50 km. Remember from Figure 2.21 that material behaves elastically only so long as it resists the stretching force; as soon as there is *any* permanent deformation, accumulated stress levels start to fall and ductile flow occurs. Ultimately, a value of accumulated stress is reached where, at the prevailing temperature conditions, quartz starts to become ductile at the base of the 18 km upper crust (in this model) and plagioclase becomes ductile at 35 km depth. This effect is visible after 10^4 years, and is becoming much more obvious after 10^5 years (Figure 2.23a), by which time stress in the elastic upper lithosphere has been amplified to 30 MPa. After 10^6 years a large ductile zone has developed in the lower crust and a smaller one at the base of the upper crust.

What, meanwhile, has been happening within the mantle?

The boundary between the ductile flow region below and the elastic region above, initially at 50 km depth, has been moving upwards. On this model, after 10^5 years, there is only a thin elastic layer from 35 to 40 km depth, right at the top of the upper mantle. After 10^6 years, this elastic layer is beginning to break down so that the whole of the mantle lithosphere is now responding by ductile flow. Stress is now focused on the elastic crustal sections between *c.* 1–12 and 18–22 km depth, but, of course, if the force were maintained for a few more million years, these too would disappear as the upper crustal ductile layer joins the growing brittle failure layer just appearing near the surface in Figure 2.23a after 10^6 years.

What do we call the stage in lithosphere rheological evolution at which no elastic zone remains but the brittle layer, moving downwards, joins the only remaining ductile layer, moving upwards?

This is the point of whole lithosphere failure, introduced in Figures 2.20 and 2.21. Perhaps you can now begin to understand why brittle failure occurs only near the surface; this is because of the **stress amplification** effect in the upper crust (i.e. this is where all the stress accumulates as the deeper lithosphere fails). The top of the upper crust is the *most* resistant zone to ductile flow, because of its low temperatures, and so sustains extremely large horizontal accumulated stresses. Here, the vertically directed pressure due to the mass of the rocks above reaches *c.* 20 MPa at 1 km depth and *c.* 125 MPa at 5 km depth. So there is an upper-crustal region where extensional shearing stresses may exceed the vertical pressure, and it is here that the rocks are most likely to fracture. Movement across such fractures causes faulting. After a long time — several million years — this brittle layer can attain a thickness of 10 km. So the general model for the rheological behaviour of the lithosphere, introduced in Figures 2.20 and 2.21, has been modified to contain several ductile–elastic transition zones, or **rheological boundaries** wherever there are major compositional changes.

While Figure 2.23a reflects the effect of time on a three-layer compositional model of the lithosphere, using the same model, Figure 2.23b explores the dimension of *variable geothermal gradient* and demonstrates convincingly the close relationship between lithosphere strength and temperature. All these models again assume a 10 MPa stretching stress operating for 1 Ma, as at the right of Figure 2.23a, for temperatures along the geotherm associated with a 60 mW m^{-2} heat flow. Notice, on these models, that the temperature at which mantle olivine becomes ductile (750 °C, see ITQ 2.7) is exceeded even at 35 km depth with heat flows of 80 and 90 mW m^{-2}. This means that there is an important crustal stress amplification effect in younger warmer lithosphere, which contrasts with average (60 mW m^{-2}) and cooler continental lithosphere.

ITQ 2.8 (a) But why, in the models to the right of Figure 2.23b, is the upper crust apparently so much stronger than the lower crust when the geothermal gradient is enhanced?

(b) Why is the brittle layer relatively thick after 1 Ma in the youngest (highest heat flow) lithosphere undergoing horizontal extensional stress?

Just to amplify the answer to ITQ 2.8, at high heat flows, temperatures are high enough throughout the lithosphere for all materials to be ductile, *except* in a near-surface zone, which is cool enough for quartz to be elastic. This zone becomes ever thinner, the higher the geothermal gradient. But any whole lithosphere stress is accumulated here, and in Figure 2.23b (right) the stress locally exceeds 160 MPa. So this upper crustal layer is bound to break up fairly rapidly by brittle fracture where the temperature stays too low for quartz to be ductile. It follows that in most regions that are, or have been, tectonically active, brittle structures are preserved in the upper crust with ductile structures at greater depths. As you will see in Block 1B and in Blocks 4–6, the problem for the structural geologist, and for those who interpret deep seismic reflection records, is to unravel the 'overprinting' effect of later structures developed in a different thermal regime from those due to initial high heat flow. In particular, in Block 5 we shall examine the critical importance of lower crustal compositions and of Moho depth in determining the strength of cool lithosphere. For example, all other things being equal, using the granulite lower crust model we have adopted (which assumes the presence of anorthite), we deduce that the crust is approximately twice as strong if the heat flow is below 60 mW m^{-2} than it is with a heat flow above 70 mW m^{-2}. When heat flow is less than 50 mW m^{-2}, the olivine rheology of the mantle becomes an important factor in lithosphere strength (see Figure 2.23b (left)). Finally, it has been shown that *with an extensional stress of 10 MPa, whole lithosphere failure will happen in periods of 1–10 Ma if the heat flow is 70 mW m^{-2} or greater,* whereas longer periods and/or larger forces are required in older lithosphere, with lower heat flow. You should be able to see that this condition is consistent with the evidence in Figure 2.23b, particularly the models presented towards the right, which we consider again in the next Section.

Summary

Taking stock of the argument as it has developed so far in Section 2.2:

1   The long-term strength of the lithosphere, defined as its ability to resist shearing stress (which is measured in the units of pressure; pascals, Pa), is governed by the dynamic viscosity of its constituent materials, where viscosity is measured in units of stress multiplied by the time taken to transmit the stress: Pa s. Estimates of dynamic viscosity vary from 10^{25} Pa s in parts of the crust and upper mantle, down to 10^{22} Pa s in the lower lithosphere (below *c.* 60 km), reaching 10^{20}–10^{21} Pa s in the asthenosphere.

2   The rheological behaviour of the lithosphere depends on the magnitude of the applied stress, the time over which it operates (Figure 2.23a), and the temperature profile, which is related to heat flow (Figure 2.23b). In the simplest model of stress accumulation (Figure 2.21), lithosphere under stress and with a uniform composition will undergo brittle fracture near the surface, where horizontal stress exceeds vertical pressure, while inelastic deformation (ductile flow) due to solid state atomic dislocations occurs at a deeper level. There may be an intermediate elastic layer (left of Figure 2.20), which, under accumulating stress, may break down to give whole lithosphere failure, as time, or stress magnitude, or indeed heat flow, is increased. Stress accumulates in elastic layer(s) because ductile flow and brittle fracture elsewhere in the lithosphere decouple the elastic zone and relieve stress in the deforming zones.

3   Strain provides a measurement of deformation in rocks, and the slowest geologically meaningful strain rate of 10^{-16} s^{-1} (producing 3% deformation in 10 Ma) defines the point at which ductile flow is considered to commence. This strain rate threshold occurs at a specific temperature for each of the common minerals; the lower the stress or the faster the strain rate, the higher the temperature required. (Figure 2.22 applies to an extensional stress of 50 MPa.)

4   A three-layer compositional model for the lithosphere under a 10 MPa extensional stress, in which the rheological properties of the upper crust depend on quartz, of the lower crust on feldspar, and of the upper mantle on olivine, is examined in detail in Figure 2.23. In most models, the cold upper crust is stronger than the lower crust, which, in turn, is stronger than the hotter mantle lithosphere, so most stress amplification occurs in the crust, particularly the upper crust. This explains the higher dynamic viscosities (see 1 above) in most of the upper lithosphere, whereas, even on low stress–low heat flow models, the lowermost lithosphere is capable of ductile flow and will exhibit lower dynamic viscosities. The models show that whole lithosphere failure, under a uniform 10 MPa extensional stress, will occur after 1 Ma if the heat flow is 90 mW m^{-2}, and after 10 Ma with a heat flow of 70 mW m^{-2}.

2.2.2 The effect of extensional and compressional stress within plates

The problem here is to determine the magnitude of the real stresses that influence the tectonic behaviour of the lithosphere. We can then apply these to the rheological models developed so far to understand the mechanical behaviour of the lithosphere under the laterally directed forces due to both extension and compression. Note that we are concerned with the stresses that break the lithosphere itself either under extension or compression rather than the stresses that move whole lithospheric plates relative to the asthenosphere (cf. Figure 2.8). The most convenient and geologically useful single parameter that can be extracted from rheological models is the **critical stress**, defined here as the level of stress required to produce whole lithosphere failure within 1 Ma.

> What would be your estimate of critical stress for the three-layer lithosphere model in Figure 2.23 if the heat flow is 80 mW m^{-2}?

Looking at Figure 2.23b, there is only a narrow elastic zone left in the 80 mW m^{-2} diagram, so the critical stress would be just greater than the stress assumed in this model, i.e. just greater than 10 MPa. It is worth emphasizing again that the calculations leading to Figure 2.23 assumed a tensile, or *extensional* stress; this is important because it transpires that *rocks are much stronger under compression than tension*. This is illustrated in Figure 2.24, which, using the same three-layer continental lithosphere, shows critical stress plotted against heat flow for both extensional and compressional regimes. Ignoring the horizontal lines for a moment, the *curves* represent the stress values at which all elastic layers break down in 1 Ma and whole lithosphere failure occurs for different values of heat flow. Table 2.3 summarizes these critical stress values with respect to heat flow and hence the age of continental lithosphere. You should satisfy yourself that you can read off the values given in the first three columns of Table 2.3 from Figure 2.24.

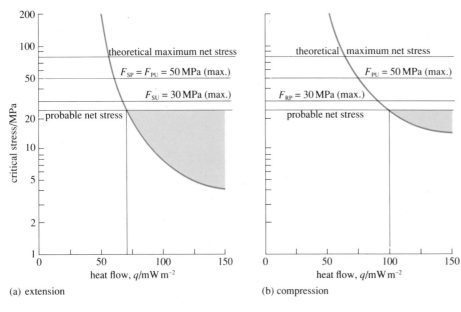

(a) extension

(b) compression

Figure 2.24 Curves for critical stress, the value of stress at which WLF occurs in 1 Ma, plotted against heat flow for (a) extensional and (b) compressional deformation. The magnitude of possible stress sources affecting continental lithosphere is indicated, together with pink areas of potential deformation, which represent that part of the diagram where heat flow is high enough at plausible stress levels for WLF to occur in 1 Ma. The lithosphere model assumed here is that described in Figure 2.23.

Table 2.3 Critical stress values and heat flows required for permanent deformation (whole lithosphere failure) of the continental lithosphere (see Figure 2.24)

Heat flow —— mW m^{-2}	Critical extensional stress/MPa	Critical compressional stress/MPa	Usual type of lithosphere (cf. ITQ 2.5 and Table 2.2)
100	8	25	tectonically active
75	20	40	<250 Ma average age
60	65	100	average continent: e.g. Palaeozoic crust
40	>200	≫200	Precambrian shield areas

Before we can make full use of the information in Table 2.3, we need to come to terms with the principal sources of stress in the lithosphere and their magnitudes. Stress can be measured directly in the uppermost crust, but, for the lower parts of the lithosphere, it is estimated by modelling the masses and strain rates involved, also by using seismic techniques. Near-surface measurements are important in all analyses of the lithospheric stress field. One technique is to employ a *strain gauge,* which records small elastic strains produced in standard materials across cavities, such as in mines or boreholes. Other methods seek to relieve the stress, such as in the use of hydraulic pressure cells, in which pressure is increased until it cancels the strain displacements created by cutting a hole or slot in the rock.

Table 2.4 Summary of principal stress generation mechanisms in the lithosphere that may be significant in tectonic deformation.

Mechanism	Symbol (cf. Figures 2.8 and 2.25)	Compression or tension	Approx. stress magnitude/MPa
subduction slab pull	F_{SP}	tension	0–50
subduction trench suction	F_{SU}	tension	0–30
ridge push	F_{RP}	compression	20–30
mantle convective drag	F_{DF}	both	1–10
lithosphere loading (plateau uplift)	F_{PU}	both, mainly tension	50 (max.)

Stresses that may be significant for deformation within the lithosphere are summarized in Table 2.4, and some are illustrated in Figure 2.25 (cf. Figure 2.8). Not surprisingly, the forces that stretch and compress the plates are the same ones as those that cause the plates to move relative to the asthenosphere. The familiar subduction *slab pull* and related *suction* forces (F_{SP} and F_{SU}) are produced by the sinking of the cold, dense lithosphere of the descending slab and may produce stresses within plates of 50 and 30 MPa, respectively. The oceanic *ridge-push* force (F_{RP}), due to positive buoyancy, helps to create tension across the ridge zone and compresses the plates to either side with stresses in the range 20–30 MPa. The mantle *drag force* (F_{DF}), acting on the base of a moving plate, is thought to be comparatively unimportant because of decoupling between the lithosphere and the asthenosphere across the low viscosity thermal boundary layer; nevertheless, this force is almost certain to have a small effect (1–10 MPa) everywhere, but whether it will be a compressional or extensional force (cf. Table 2.1) will depend on the relative directions of plate and asthenosphere motion. Finally, loading stresses (Figure 2.25c) are produced where the lithosphere is loaded by surface topography, as in mountain ranges, or by lateral density variations.

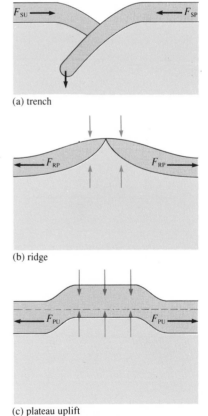

(a) trench

(b) ridge

(c) plateau uplift

Figure 2.25 Origin of the main lithosphere driving forces derived mainly from density contrasts at plate boundaries (a) and (b) and in areas of topographic uplift (c). In (b) and (c), the topographic load is isostatically compensated by lower density asthenosphere. The vertical arrows denote gravitational and isostatic forces, and the horizontal arrows show derived lithospheric stress.

> For example, what would be the additional vertical stress due to a 2 km high mountain of materials with a density 2.5 Mg m^{-3} ($\rho = 2\,500$ kg m^{-3}; pressure $= \rho g h$ where h is height and g, the acceleration due to gravity is approximately 10 m s^{-2}).

The vertical stress would be 2 500 kg m^{-3} × 10 m s^{-2} × 2 000 km $= 50 × 10^6$ kg m^{-1} s$^{-2} = 50$ MPa, and in the situation shown in Figure 2.25c, this downwards directed gravitational force is isostatically compensated by lower-density material at depth in the mantle. The downwards gravitational and upwards isostatic forces therefore combine to produce lateral tensional stresses across elevated regions, such as continental collision zones and passive continental margins where continental and oceanic lithosphere are adjacent, and this is known as the **plateau uplift force** (F_{PU}). It also produces compression in the lithosphere to either side, and, because the lithosphere is rigid, the entire downwards force can be transmitted laterally, so F_{PU} may reach 50 MPa.

In summary, the major sources of lithospheric stress that are of tectonic significance arise from forces due to density contrasts at different types of plate boundaries and regions of continental uplift. Their magnitude, and the build up of stress across the lithosphere may be modified by other forces (due to transform faults, collision zones, etc.) and by thermal and bending stresses, but these are often of minor significance, being rapidly dissipated over geological time-scales.

So what are the implications of these stresses for deformation? We can now return to Figure 2.24a, in which you will see that the two principal extensional forces on *continental* lithosphere (F_{SU} and F_{PU} — values in Table 2.4) combine to give a theoretical maximum net stress of 80 MPa. Note that in certain circumstances F_{SP} can act on a continental plate (see, for example, Figure 2.27), but this force normally only acts on oceanic lithosphere between a ridge and a trench (Figure 2.25a). F_{RP} can only act in compression, affecting continents where they are attached to oceans via passive continental margins. So F_{SU} and F_{PU} are the main extensional forces that affect continental lithosphere, and it is extremely unlikely that both would combine with their individual maximum values operating in the same direction within a plate. A more realistic net stress is c. 25 MPa. From Figure 2.24a, this critical stress defines a minimum heat flow of 70 mW m^{-2} at which whole lithosphere failure can occur by internal stress amplification within 1 Ma. Of course, the stress values in Table 2.4 apply uniformly across the lithosphere, but are amplified in the way we described earlier as the lithosphere approaches failure. The minimum heat flow of 70 mW m^{-2} does not imply that extension cannot occur at lower heat flows; merely it indicates that such deformation is less likely because it will take longer due to greater lithosphere strength. Thus we arrive at an area in the critical stress–heat flow diagram where there is a high potential for extensional deformation.

> Over what age span of continental lithosphere do you think we would be most likely to find evidence of extensional basin formation today?

Clearly, by reference to Table 2.3, a critical heat flow of 70 mW m^{-2} will include all Mesozoic and Tertiary lithosphere and perhaps some of the warmer Palaeozoic provinces — and that deduction is borne out exactly by observations of young extensional basins (Figure 2.26). All the Precambrian shield areas in Figure 2.26 do not reach the critical heat flow value of 70 mW m^{-2}. In South India, for example, where mean heat flow is 50 mW m^{-2}, the critical stress for whole lithosphere failure would be c. 150 MPa and clearly this is not being attained.

> But what about the zones of Palaeozoic crust? What would be the critical stress for each of these regions?

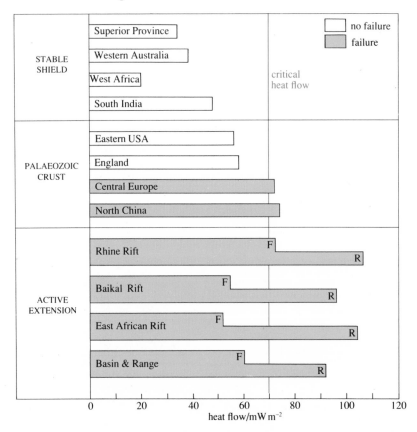

Figure 2.26 Mean heat flow values for a number of tectonic regions grouped into Precambrian stable shields, zones affected by Palaeozoic tectonic processes, and areas of active extensional rifting. Regions undergoing failure have columns exceeding the critical heat flow value of 70 mW m^{-2} for deformation at plausible lithospheric stress (Figure 2.24a). For regions undergoing active extension, both rift (R) and flank (F) heat flows are given.

The eastern USA and English provinces, with heat flow of c. 60 mW m^{-2} would require a critical stress of 65 MPa (Table 2.3), whereas Central Europe and North China, with heat flow of c. 75 mW m^{-2}, require a critical stress of 20 MPa. The fact that the latter two provinces are undergoing extensional failure, whereas the former are not, gives us some confidence that both our compositional model of the lithosphere and our analysis of lithospheric stress are broadly correct. The four zones of active extension (Figure 2.26, bottom) have much higher heat flow values associated with rifting. No doubt heat flow is elevated by adiabatic rise of hot asthenosphere beneath these regions, but in their present thermal state, it appears that extension will continue even at very low stress levels, a subject to which we return in Section 2.2.3.

We now consider what happens to the continental lithosphere under compression. The theoretical maximum net stress produced by a combination of F_{PU} and F_{RP}, where ridge push is transmitted via the oceanic lithosphere through a passive continental margin, is again 80 MPa. Again, however, such high values of overall lithospheric stress are unlikely, and a more realistic value of compressional stress is c. 25 MPa. However, the greater strength of the lithosphere under compression (Figure 2.24b) means that a critical heat flow of 100 mW m^{-2} would be required to produce significant deformation. Such a high heat flow is currently only found in the hottest tectonically active regions (Table 2.3), most of which are currently undergoing extension rather than compression! Rheological modelling therefore predicts that *major compressional deformation should not normally occur within plates*. This is exactly what we observe, a fact that may surprise you, given the evidence for compressional tectonics in places like the Alps and Himalayas. But these were places where the continental parts of two *separate* lithospheric plates, at least one of which was already moving under tension, came together and collided (e.g. Figure 2.27). So compressional deformation in the Earth's continental lithosphere is restricted to convergent plate boundaries where large-scale collision-resistance forces may lead to complex overthrusting and uplift processes.

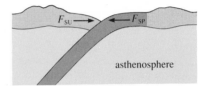

Figure 2.27 Schematic illustration of forces operating at an active continental margin where two continental masses will collide. That on the right is attached to a piece of ocean lithosphere being subducted beneath the continent on the left.

All the comments above have been focused on the rheological behaviour of the continental lithosphere. But as you will appreciate from Table 2.4, similar stresses operate on oceanic lithosphere. The major forces operating on the oceanic lithosphere are F_{SP} and F_{RP}, which, together, provide a potential maximum stress of 80 MPa. Now this brings us to an extremely important point — can you see that F_{RP} and F_{SP} both operate in the same direction, F_{RP} pushing from an ocean ridge and F_{SP} pulling from a subduction zone? Look back to Figure 2.8 if you have any doubts. What this means is that *the total force that makes the oceanic lithosphere move relative to the asthenosphere is the combination of F_{RP} and F_{SP}.* But this is not the same problem that we have been considering in this Section, where the lithospheric plate itself fails either under extension or compression.

> Suppose F_{RP} and F_{SP} both operate on the same piece of oceanic plate, in the same direction, and at their maximum values. What will be the extensional stress across the lithosphere that could cause internal deformation?

From Table 2.4, F_{SP} reaches a maximum of 50 MPa whereas F_{RP} reaches only 30 MPa, so the extensional stress *within* the lithosphere under these circumstances would be c. 20 MPa. This serves to emphasize two points: first, as with compression in the continents, we should not be surprised to find that most tectonic activity in the oceans occurs at plate margins where there are much greater stress *differences* than within plates; second, the probable net stress within oceanic lithosphere is unlikely to be much greater than the 25 MPa we used in the continental case (cf. Figure 2.24). So, how easy is it to create permanent deformation within oceanic lithosphere?

> **ITQ 2.9** Given that the oceanic lithosphere is dominated by the rheological properties of olivine in the mantle part, and by plagioclase in the top 10 km, will it be stronger or weaker than continental lithosphere under the influence of the same geothermal gradient and stress regime?

In fact, the threshold temperature for ductile behaviour in olivine (750 °C) occurs at about 70 km depth on the normal oceanic lithosphere geotherm (Figure 2.9). Material above this depth will behave elastically, and it will take much longer, with much greater stress amplification than in continental lithosphere, for critical stress values to be attained. It follows that critical stress–heat flow curves for oceanic lithosphere would be displaced towards the top right of Figure 2.24 so that unrealistically high values of critical stress would be required to produce within-plate deformation. Ocean ridges themselves are, of course, regions of particularly high heat flow, originally developed in most cases during continental lithosphere extension but propagated by the continuing large differential stresses across the plate boundary.

2.2.3 The evolution of strength during deformation

We have seen that the bulk strength of the lithosphere depends on the proportions of quartz, feldspar and olivine-rich material. The critical stress required for whole lithosphere failure depends on all components and their temperatures, particularly on the strongest layer, which remains elastic until, finally, it yields when the lithosphere breaks. Remember that all the continental rheological models we have discussed included a 35 km thick quartz–feldspar crust and a 65 km thick olivine-rich mantle. By analogy with our deductions about oceanic lithosphere strength, it must follow that if the continental lithosphere is *thinned* by extensional deformation, with time it will become *stronger*. This is largely because, once the extended lithosphere section has reached thermal equilibrium (Figure 2.28), there will be less crust and more olivine-rich mantle in the section. Bringing into the top 35 km (where temperatures are less than 750 °C) more olivine, with higher strength than, say, feldspar in the temperature interval 425–750 °C (Figure 2.22), must radically strengthen the region just above 35 km, hence strengthening the entire lithosphere. Similarly, if the lithosphere is thickened and incorporates a thicker crust (Figure 2.31), the deep zone of mantle olivine will easily become ductile under stress, so the stress is then amplified more within the crust. However, the region in which the crustal minerals have effectively replaced mantle minerals is now weaker; the whole lithosphere will therefore fail more rapidly: *thickening weakens the lithosphere*.

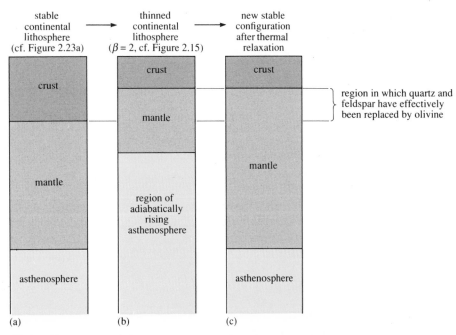

Figure 2.28 Stages in the evolution of a continental lithosphere profile, starting (a) with a configuration similar to Figure 2.23a and (b) undergoing symmetrical thinning with a stretch factor of 2 as in Figure 2.15, and then relaxing thermally (c) back to a total thickness of 100 km. Topographic anomalies produced by stretching are ignored here, but are illustrated in Figure 2.29.

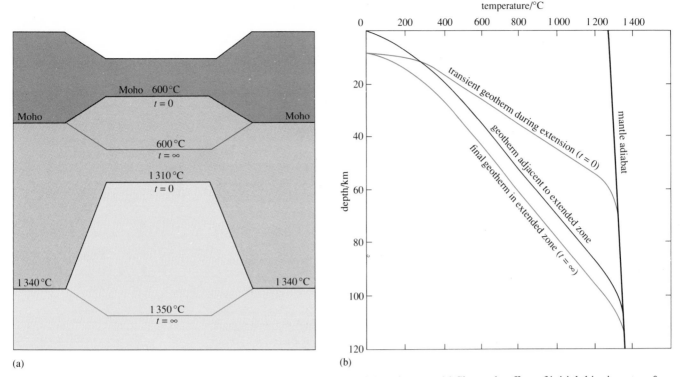

Figure 2.29 Extension ($\beta = 2$) of the continental lithosphere at high initial strain rates. (a) Shows the effect of initial thinning at $t = 0$ where the isotherms are bunched upwards due to adiabatic rise of asthenosphere (1 310 °C at c. 50 km depth). The red lines indicate new isotherms after thermal relaxation ($t = \infty$) has strengthened the lithosphere. (b) Shows temperature profiles associated with extension ($t = 0$) and thermal relaxation ($t = \infty$) in the extended zone.

Of course, the evolution of strength *during* deformation is a great deal more complicated because the whole thermal structure of the lithosphere changes. First we shall examine extension, a process which may actually result in two opposing effects on different time-scales: (i) a steepening of the geotherm through the ascent of hot asthenospheric material, which must initially weaken the lithosphere (Figure 2.28b), and (ii) a thinning of the crust, which, as we have seen (Figure 2.28c), will act to strengthen the lithosphere after cooling. Figure 2.29 illustrates the extension process at high strain rates ($10^{-14}\,\text{s}^{-1}$ and faster) where the lithosphere is thinned more rapidly than it can regain thermal equilibrium. In this case, initially (i.e. immediately after extension; $t = 0$), the isotherms beneath the zone of stretching are packed together, and you can see that both the 600 °C and 1 310 °C (adiabatic) isotherms have moved closer to the surface in Figure 2.29a. The result is that the geothermal gradient and heat flow are increased so that a **transient geotherm** with high $\Delta T/z$ is produced (Figure 2.29b). It follows that the strength of the lithosphere *decreases during stretching*: this is known as **strain softening**. Assuming that the stretching force is then removed, perhaps because the related tectonic movements have been accommodated, then the extensional stress is reduced. After reaching a maximum, strain rates will start to decline. As the newly attenuated lithosphere cools towards thermal equilibrium (a process known as **thermal relaxation**), it starts to strengthen, and, because of crustal thinning, it will exceed its initial strength some time before reaching thermal equilibrium at $t = \infty$. Notice that the high strain rates, which we have assumed in Figure 2.29, *if perpetuated,* are quite capable of rifting apart the continental crust with adiabatic rise of partially molten asthenosphere right to the surface, forming basaltic oceanic crust.

> But what about extension at lower strain rates? How might lithosphere temperatures and strength evolve under these conditions?

If extension takes place slowly, the base of the lithosphere may have time to re-equilibrate during stretching so that the transient geotherm is not displaced to the extent shown in Figure 2.29b. In the limiting case of the slowest geologically meaningful strain rates, approaching $10^{-16}\,\text{s}^{-1}$, there is no transient geotherm, and the base of the lithosphere will move downwards continuously keeping pace with the thinning effect.

What will this do to the evolution of lithosphere strength during extension?

As the crust thins and the isotherms are displaced (e.g. the 600 °C isotherm in Figure 2.29a moves from the Moho to well into the upper mantle, as shown at $t = \infty$), the lithosphere will progressively strengthen: this is known as **strain hardening**. This is equivalent to moving straight from the left to right of Figure 2.28 (i.e. from a to c) — remember: at *low* strain rates. It will be fairly obvious that if the lithosphere strengthens progressively during slow extension, the process must be self-limiting; in other words, extension zones can only reach a limiting stretch factor, β, before extension stops because strength has increased. This is illustrated in Figure 2.30a, which shows that for strain rates of 10^{-15} to $10^{-16}\,s^{-1}$, the applied stress must *increase* dramatically in order for β to exceed 1.5. For example, for an initial stress of 45 MPa in this model (60 mW m^{-2} heat flow geotherm), extension may commence with a slow strain rate of $10^{-16}\,s^{-1}$. To maintain extension, however, the stress required climbs rapidly to 200 MPa because strain hardening has taken place during initial extension. In contrast, if there is a *larger* initial stress, then strain rates of 10^{-13} to $10^{-14}\,s^{-1}$ may occur, and, if perpetuated, *strain softening* leads to *decreased* stress being required for continued extension past this point. The consequences for the evolution of heat flow through extension zones (Figure 2.30b) are for heat flow to be enhanced at high strain rates and to be slightly reduced at low strain rates. (Note that the initial conditions follow the 60 mW m^{-2} geotherm.) The change from strain hardening to strain softening occurs between the strain rate curves for 10^{-14} and $10^{-15}\,s^{-1}$, and it is useful to consider how long a given extension takes to occur at these rates.

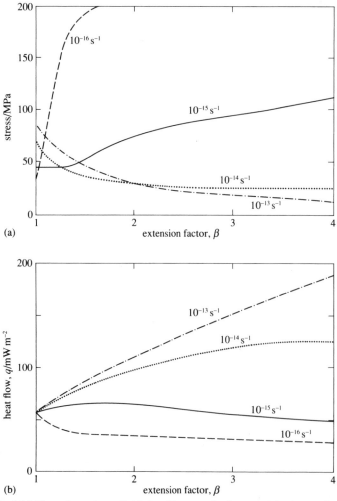

Figure 2.30 (a) Lithosphere strength, defined here as the force required to maintain a given strain rate, and (b) surface heat flow plotted against β, the lithosphere extension factor, for a range of strain rates 10^{-13} to $10^{-16}\,s^{-1}$. The initial model assumes a heat flow of only 60 mW m^{-2}, so that the critical stress (cf. Figure 2.24a) is rather large, but a similar set of curves could be produced at lower initial stress and higher initial heat flow. Notice that strain rates of 10^{-13} to $10^{-14}\,s^{-1}$ evolve towards strain-softening and higher heat flow as extension continues, whereas strain rates of 10^{-15} to $10^{-16}\,s^{-1}$ strain harden after β reaches c. 1.5.

How long will it take for 50% extension ($\beta = 1.5$) to occur at strain rates of 10^{-14} and 10^{-15} s^{-1}?

From equation 2.6, the time taken ($t = l/LS$) is given by the fractional extension ($l/L = 0.5$) divided by the strain rate ($S = 1 \times 10^{-14}$ s^{-1}), giving 5×10^{13} s or 1.6 Ma. At 10^{-15} s^{-1}, the time taken is *c.* 16 Ma. So the boundary between strain softening and strain hardening, which occurs between these two strain rates, leads us to conclude that *extension zones that form in less than 10 Ma, and preferably in less than 1 Ma will be self-propagating, with decreasing lithospheric strength, whereas those taking 10 Ma or more to form will strain harden and be self-limiting at about 50% extension.* Looking back to Figure 2.29, we hope you can now see that extensions at high strain rates, such as that which produced the transient geotherm, would continue unless the stress causing extension was removed. In the case illustrated, this must have happened for thermal relaxation to have occurred. Interestingly, most intra-continental extensional basins do have limited extension, with an average β value of 1.4–1.5 suggesting that they are preserved in this state either because stress declines after initial extension or because strain rates never become great enough for strain softening to occur. Of course, it is highly likely that once past *c.* 50% extension, an extension zone will become self-propagating at low stress and so form an ocean ridge. Exactly what happens must depend on the local stress regime, but you should note that two intra-continental basins with high β values are the North Sea ($\beta = 1.6$–1.9) and the Basin and Range Province of the western USA ($\beta = 1.5$–2.0). Both are mentioned in the video programme (VC 271) *Extensional Tectonics* and the formation mechanism of the latter is discussed in Section 3.2, which is the best point for you to view this programme.

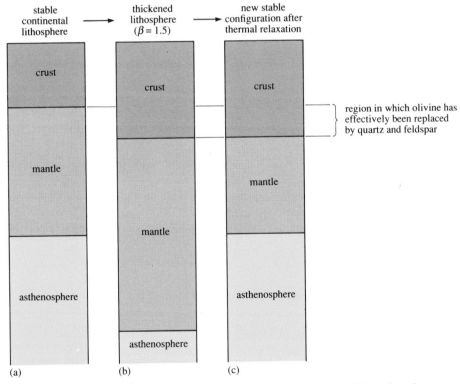

Figure 2.31 Stages in the evolution of a continental lithosphere profile undergoing compression. Starting (a) with a configuration as in Figure 2.15; (b) after thickening ($\beta = 1.5$) at rapid strain rates (allowing no time for thermal equilibration), and (c) after thermal relaxation back to a 100 km thickness. Topographic anomalies produced by compression are illustrated in Figure 2.32.

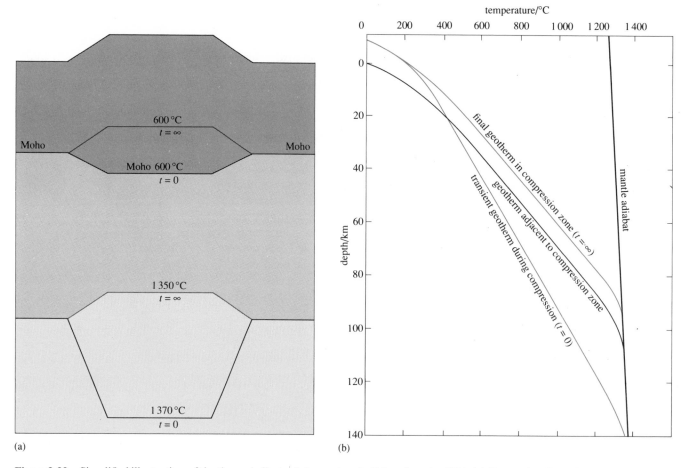

Figure 2.32 Simplified illustration of the thermal effects of shortening the lithosphere by 50%. (a) Shows the effect of initial thickening at $t=0$, where isotherms are spread down to a 1 370 °C temperature on the adiabat at 150 km depth. The red lines indicate new isotherms after thermal relaxation ($t=\infty$). (b) Shows temperature profiles associated with compression ($t=0$) and thermal relaxation ($t=\infty$) in the compressed zone.

ITQ 2.10   Following the same lines of reasoning through a much simpler case, you are now in a position to consider what happens to strength during lithospheric *compression* leading to crustal shortening and thickening (cf. Figure 2.31). Figure 2.32 gives a 50% thickening model with isotherms and geotherms.

(a)   From Figure 2.32, what will be the result of compressive deformation at the high strain rate assumed in this model? In particular, does this lead to initial strain hardening or softening?

(b)   What do you think will happen if there are slow strain rates, whereby thermal equilibrium is maintained?

Earlier, in relation to Figure 2.31, we concluded that thickening weakens the lithosphere. Although this is quite true after thermal relaxation, ITQ 2.10 and Figure 2.32 show that initial compressive deformation at high strain rates serves to strengthen the lithosphere. The high initial stresses required to promote compressional deformation (Figure 2.24b) together with this strain hardening effect during deformation on geologically meaningful time-scales mean that *we would not expect much large-scale shortening within the lithosphere* (more than, say, 30–50%). Indeed, as noted earlier, most compressive deformation of the lithosphere is confined to plate boundaries — collision zones — where the vast majority of tectonic uplift processes have occurred in the geological record. Here the complex interthrusting of crustal and mantle layers in different thermal states combine to produce a much more complicated picture than we have developed so far. The particular cases of the Scottish Caledonides and Himalayas will be used to illustrate some of these complexities in Blocks 4 and 6.

Finally, as with the basin evolution model we met in Section 2.1.2 (see Figure 2.15), continental mountains resulting from compressive deformation have initial uplift rates that can be measured to evaluate strain rates and model lithosphere rheology beneath collision zones. Once mountains have been produced, there is topographic decay due to surface erosion, coupled with lateral flow in ductile zones within the lower crust and mantle (e.g. Figure 2.33). In this way, the thickness of deep continental roots is reduced and *the seismic depth to the Moho reaches a surprisingly uniform level (35–40 km) beneath most continental areas*. This is an essentially isostatic process whereby ductile flow beneath zones of anomalous excess mass progressively reduces both the mass and topographic anomalies. Note that in Figure 2.33 the extra mass of the upper crust is 'compensated' by a deep low density continental 'root'; there may also be an upwards bulge in the low density asthenosphere under such zones as illustrated in Figure 2.25c. The force F_{PU} resulting from the topographic load will tend to create extension across the mountainous zone as we discussed earlier.

In a qualitative way, you should be able to see that the time-scale over which subsidence of uplifted zones occurs can be used to calculate the dynamic viscosity of lithosphere components. For example, decay often occurs on time-scales of about 100 Ma, and this leads to a low value of viscosity ($c.$ 10^{21} Pa s) in the lower crust and uppermost mantle compared with 10^{25} Pa s in the upper crust. This low value probably results from the high temperatures there *after* thermal relaxation (Figure 2.32b). These reduce the viscosity and allow the highly ductile material to flow laterally, thus reducing the topography and depth to Moho, and, by cooling, increasing the viscosity to normal levels (10^{22} Pa s and higher — cf. beginning of Section 2.2) at which point lateral flow rates reduce. So we see that once crustal material reaches depths greater than 35–40 km, it tends to become unstable and is subject to basal flow and mass redistribution (though there are exceptions to this generalization). We hope you can see, therefore, that the thickness of the continental crust, like those of the oceanic and continental lithospheres depends on the temperature profile, which controls its strength, and is therefore related to the value of heat flow at the surface. The lithosphere and its component layers are dynamic systems in which composition, strength (viscosity), temperature and deformation behaviour are all interdependent. This is a complex subject, and we hope you have followed at least some of the arguments so far and that you have begun to understand some of the answers to the question: 'What is the lithosphere?'.

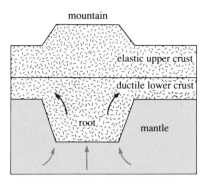

Figure 2.33 Schematic model for the decay of mountain roots, hence surface topography, with time due to flow in ductile layers, in this case within the lower crust and upper mantle.

Summary

In Sections 2.2.2 and 2.2.3, we have examined the consequences of extensional and compressional stress for deformation *within* plates. Remember that the same stresses cause whole plates to move relative to the asthenosphere because of ductile flow in the latter, but here we are concerned with the development of brittle and ductile layers *within* stressed lithosphere which brings about whole lithosphere failure.

1   The sources of stress within the lithosphere, summarized in Table 2.4 and Figure 2.25, lead to theoretical maxima of $c.$ 80 MPa across the whole lithosphere both under extension and compression. Given that most of this stress is accommodated by wholesale movement of the plates and is dissipated at plate boundaries, the maximum likely value of net within-plate stress is thought to be $c.$ 25 MPa, again both under extension and compression.

2   Using a critical stress (the stress required to produce whole lithosphere failure in 1 Ma) versus heat flow diagram (Figure 2.24) and a three-layer continental lithosphere model with a 35 km thick crust, if the critical stress is 25 MPa, the minimum heat flow required for permanent extension is 70 mW m^{-2} and for permanent compressional deformation is 100 mW m^{-2}. The difference is due to the fact that rocks are much stronger under compressional than extensional stress. The relationship between critical stress and heat flow with respect to the age of the continental lithosphere is summarized in Table 2.3. From this, we deduce that normal continental lithosphere of Palaeozoic and particularly of Mesozoic/Tertiary age may deform by extension (cf. Figure 2.26) but that within-plate compressional deformation should be rare.

3   Oceanic lithosphere is stronger than continental lithosphere because of the thinner oceanic crust, and this means that olivine, which resists deformation at

higher temperatures than quartz and feldspar, occurs in cooler zones, closer to the surface. So within-plate deformation is comparatively rare in the oceans except where there are very large stresses (e.g. across ocean ridges) or rising thermal plumes from the deeper mantle which weaken the plate.

4   The evolution of lithosphere strength during deformation depends on the strain rate. If deformation is relatively rapid, with strain rates of 10^{-13} to $10^{-14}\,\mathrm{s}^{-1}$, then thermal equilibrium cannot be maintained and transient geotherms are established (see, for example, Figures 2.29b and 2.32b). Under these circumstances ($t=0$), *extended* continental lithosphere is weakened, or strain softened, and if extensional stress is perpetuated, decreasing values of stress are required for large stretch factors to result (cf. Figure 2.30a); the result of such large stretch factors is that new oceanic lithosphere may then develop between two previously joined continents. In *compression,* high strain rates lead to strain hardening of the continental lithosphere, mainly because the transient geotherm is associated with lower temperatures. Clearly, compressional deformation is a self-limiting process.

5   If deformation is relatively slow, with strain rates of 10^{-15} to $10^{-16}\,\mathrm{s}^{-1}$, thermal equilibrium is maintained and conditions result that are identical to those after thermal relaxation under high strain rates ($t=\infty$ in Figures 2.29 and 2.32). These involve an overall strengthening of the continental lithosphere after extension and an overall weakening after compression. This reflects the relative proportions of crustal (weaker in the 425–750 °C temperature range) and mantle mineralogy in the deformed lithosphere. In turn, the changes are due to the migration of the crust–mantle boundary, upwards in extension and downwards in compression (cf. Figures 2.28c and 2.31c).

6   The overall rates of vertical movement during and after deformation can be used to deduce the viscosity of the component layers in the lithosphere, giving broad agreement with the values quoted in Section 2.2.1 (Summary, point 1). Interestingly, topographic anomalies resulting from compressional deformation produce ductile, low viscosity lower crust (Figure 2.33), which flows laterally, gradually reducing the anomaly and increasing lower crustal viscosity: thus continental crustal thickness tends towards a uniform value of 35–40 km. But thinned crust is resistant to change, because while mountains can be eroded, basins cannot, and the lower crust is shallower and therefore cooler.

The processes and constraints on lithosphere deformation introduced here will be developed in relation to case studies of particular areas both within and at the boundaries of plates in the next Section and, in much more detail, in the remainder of this Course. We hope that the sequence of case studies will help to consolidate your understanding of this first Section and that you will find the Summaries particularly helpful as you read on.

SAQs FOR SECTION 2

SAQ 2.1   (a)   Equations 2.1 and 2.2 express the relationship between heat flow (q, in W m^{-2}), depth of ocean (d, in metres) and age of the oceanic lithosphere (t, in Ma):

$$q = Ct^{-0.5} \ (2.1) \quad \text{and} \quad d = Kt^{0.5} \ (2.2)$$

(i) Explain why equation 2.1 has a minus sign whereas 2.2 has not.

(ii) What is the physical significance of C and K?

(iii) What are the units of C and K?

(iv) Qualitatively, what would be the significance for oceanic lithosphere thickness if K were twice the commonly observed value: 350 in the units deduced in (iii)?

(b) To what extent do these equations provide a sound description of the observed behaviour of the whole oceanic lithosphere?

SAQ 2.2   Explain briefly how the plate model and boundary layer model for the oceanic lithosphere differ in the way they account for the decline in heat flow observed with age. Which model accounts most satisfactorily for the physical behaviour of the oceanic lithosphere?

SAQ 2.3 What features of (a) the large-scale gravity field over the oceans and (b) the stress regime affecting oceanic plates suggest that rising thermal plumes are not a necessary feature of the upper mantle beneath oceanic spreading ridges?

SAQ 2.4 (a) Explain in terms of the geotherms shown in Figure 2.9 and 2.12 how we define the depth of the boundary between the lithosphere and asthenosphere.

(b) Compare the continental geotherm for a heat flow of 100 mW m^{-2} (Figure 2.12), which would be typical for a 60 Ma old province, with the oceanic geotherm for 60 Ma (Figure 2.9). Why is the continental lithosphere less thick than oceanic lithosphere at this particular age, and what evidence is there from continental heat flow studies that supports your explanation?

(c) Why were continental lithosphere thicknesses (using our modern definition of lithosphere) associated with low values of heat flow probably overestimated by the Pollack and Chapman model? Can you give *two* reasons?

SAQ 2.5 Which of the following statements are true and which false? Briefly explain your answers.

(a) If $q^* = 0.6\bar{q}$ and the mean heat flow in a continental heat flow province is 50 mW m^{-2}, the lithosphere will be $c.$ 130 km thick. (Assume a 10 km radiothermal layer and uniform thermal conductivity of 3.0 W m^{-1} K^{-1}.)

(b) Xenoliths from kimberlite pipes contain mineral assemblages that equilibrated at P–T conditions close to the 40 mW m^{-2} geotherm in Figure 2.12, thus showing that the 90 Ma old mantle beneath S Africa is thermally anomalous.

(c) Regions of continental extension are subject to subsidence on two counts: first, tectonic subsidence directly related to stretching, and second, thermal subsidence due to contraction of the warm asthenosphere that rose beneath the stretched zone.

(d) The seismic low velocity zone is associated with seismic wave attenuation, and is caused by the local reduction of elastic moduli at some depth in the mantle, usually because of partial melting.

(e) Although the asthenosphere and low velocity layer are often coincident, the former is defined by the mantle's response to long-term elastic deformation whereas the latter is defined using short-term plastic properties.

(f) The tectosphere concept of Jordan recognizes that the lithosphere of continental shield areas may have had a thermal and tectonic history in common with that of the subjacent asthenospheric mantle down to 400 km.

SAQ 2.6 (a) What is the distinction between elastic and inelastic deformation as applied to the crystalline material of the Earth's lithosphere?

(b) How do the definitions of the asthenosphere and the low velocity layer relate to elastic and inelastic deformation?

(c) How is the *strength* of lithosphere materials, as described by their dynamic viscosity, related to elastic and inelastic deformation?

SAQ 2.7 Explain as briefly as you can what is meant by the following terms:
(a) brittle deformation,
(b) ductile deformation,
(c) whole lithosphere failure,
(d) critical stress (as defined in this Block).

SAQ 2.8 In 2–3 sentences each, try to account for the following observations:

(a) Within-plate compressional deformation is rare in comparison with extensional deformation, and where it does occur, only a small amount of crustal shortening is found.

(b) Stress dissipation at plate boundaries is much greater than that resulting from within-plate deformation.

(c) The depth of the Moho beneath continental areas is remarkably uniform at $c.$ 35–40 km.

3 LITHOSPHERE BOUNDARY PROCESSES: SOME CASE STUDIES

The evolution of the continental lithosphere and the processes that affect it have been the subject of debate for over a century. Early workers conceived of **geosynclines**; the down-warping of continental crust to form elongated sedimentary basins, which were filled with sediments and then folded and uplifted to form young mountain chains. The theory of plate tectonics replaced this model with one of large rigid plates, the interactions between which shaped the continental blocks. Classic models of geosynclines refer to the processes occurring in either ocean basins of restricted width during closure, or in marginal basins behind island arcs (Section 3.2.1) where sedimentation rates are high and where the material will become incorporated into a continental mass once the ocean basin closes. More important, recently, it has been recognized that the continents are being *continuously reworked* by tectonic forces and that large areas of continental crust were not formed *in situ* but have moved large distances before arriving at their present locations.

Many of these tectonic processes occur at or near plate boundaries, and, as you know, many of the older portions of continental lithosphere are generally cooler, more stable and relatively resistant to reworking. In Blocks 2–4, we shall be examining the range of tectonic and consequent geological processes occurring at divergent, extensional boundaries under low strain rates (Block 2), convergent compressional ocean–continent boundaries (Block 3) and convergent continent–continent boundaries (Block 4). The purpose of this Section is to explain some simple examples of lithosphere boundary processes as a prelude to the more detailed examination in later Blocks. We shall use examples mainly from the well-studied areas of Western North America, concluding with revision of the tectonic structure of the British Isles. The latter will introduce you to aspects of the lithospheric evolution of Britain prior to our study of its deep geophysical structure in Block 1B.

3.1 PLATE BOUNDARIES AND THEIR MIGRATION

So far, we have been discussing the movement of plates away from extension zones and towards convergence zones, and in Figures 2.8 and 2.25, we considered the sources of stress that both make the plates move and cause deformation within plates. But to understand the mechanical evolution of plate boundaries, we need to know about the relative speed and direction of movement of adjacent plates: we need **plate movement vectors**. As you may recall from earlier courses, one of the best methods of measuring plate motions is to use magnetic anomaly patterns over the oceanic lithosphere. The spacing of the magnetic anomalies, when referred to the magnetic polarity time-scale, gives us a distance moved in a given time, in other words a speed and direction (since spreading is normal to the magnetic anomalies), hence a plate movement vector. However, as you may also remember, this technique only gives us a measurement of the *relative* motion between the plates (e.g. relative motion to either side of a spreading ridge). When we want to consider the *absolute* motion of the plates with respect to fixed coordinates, matters become a shade more complicated.

> **ITQ 3.1** For example, consider a fairly familiar situation as shown in Figure 3.1. This is a section through the Earth from the Atlantic Ocean, through Africa to the Indian Ocean. The average relative spreading rates for the Mid-Atlantic Ridge and the Carlsberg Ridge are given.
>
> (a) and (b) For each of the following situations estimate (i) the relative speeds, and (ii) the directions of plate motion for the African Plate.
>
> (a) American Plate fixed
>
> (b) Australian Plate fixed
>
> (c) Suppose, instead, that the African Plate is fixed in an absolute frame of reference. What does this tell you about the nature of absolute plate movements associated with the two ocean ridges?

This example shows, very convincingly, that *plate margins themselves move with time,* and since Africa really is almost stationary in an absolute frame of reference

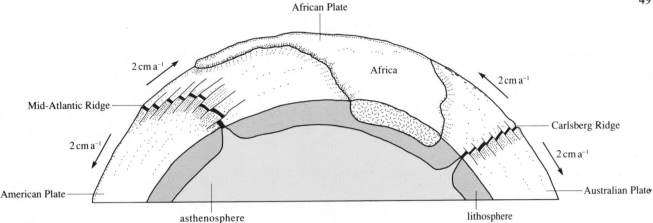

Figure 3.1 Section through the Earth from the Atlantic ridge through Africa to the Carlsberg ridge in the Indian Ocean (for use with ITQ 3.1).

(details in Block 2), both adjacent oceanic ridges *must* themselves be moving. Notice also that the African Plate is growing in size as these divergent boundaries have moved outwards, and this leads to a second important conclusion: *that some plates are also moving relative to the mantle below.* In view of our earlier discussions about the nature of processes beneath ocean ridges (Section 2.1.1) and the stresses that move the lithosphere relative to the asthenosphere (Section 2.2.2), you should not find this conclusion too surprising.

But how do we set about the task of measuring the *absolute* speed and direction of plate motion?

There are several techniques; for example, it may be assumed that a certain plate or plate boundary is stationary so that absolute motions of the other plates can be determined from this assumption (as in ITQ 3.1a and b). But, as ITQ 3.1 demonstrated, this technique is only as good as the inherent assumption, and by far the most successful technique is the use of *hot spots,* which underlie certain volcanic areas. Sometimes these are coincident with plate boundaries (e.g. the unusually active ocean ridge zones of the Azores, Galapagos Islands and Iceland), while others produce volcanism within plates (e.g. the Emperor–Hawaiian seamount volcanic island chain of the NW Pacific — Figure 3.2a). Hot spots are presumed, for a variety of geophysical reasons, to have almost stationary *sublithospheric magma sources* over which the plates migrate. It follows that the ages and distances between volcanoes produced by the same hot spot give a measure of absolute plate motion (Figure 3.2b). There are two notes of caution, however; first, some apparent hot spots have been identified that may have resulted from within-plate extension, producing passive rifts (cf. Section 2.1.1; also Block 2) above zones of adiabatically rising asthenosphere. Second, it is known that hot spots themselves migrate with time relative to a notional fixed mantle reference frame; fortunately, this migration is at speeds an order of magnitude slower than plate motions. There are several major long-lived hot spots, however, relative to which a self-consistent set of absolute plate motion vectors has now been established, and some of these are shown in Figure 3.3.

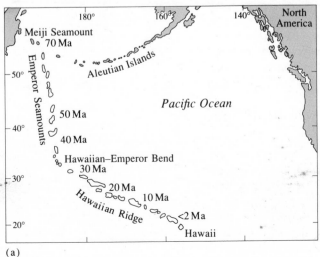

Figure 3.2 (a) The Emperor–Hawaiian seamount volcanic island chain of the NW Pacific showing the progression of ages (in Ma) from northwest to southeast. (b) Schematic cross-section illustrating the formation of volcanic island chains by movement of oceanic lithosphere over a fixed hot-spot in the deeper mantle.

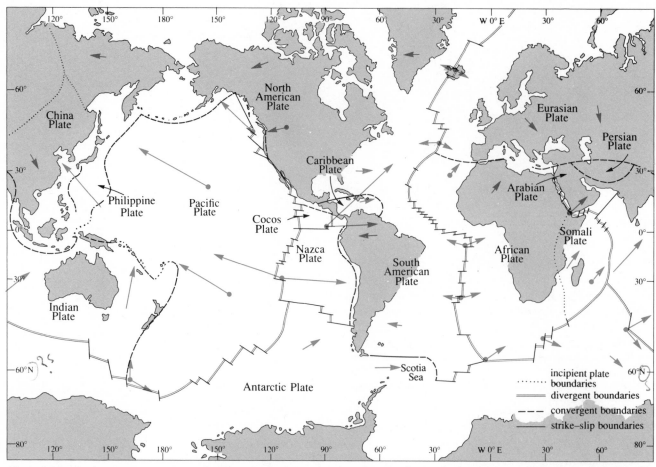

Figure 3.3 Absolute movement vectors for lithospheric plates related to a hot spot frame of reference (some of the hot spots used in this analysis are marked as red dots). Ocean ridge/transform fault systems are in solid lines; convergent boundaries are in dashed lines. Length of red arrows indicates relative magnitude of plate velocities; directions of motion are along arrows. Where two arrows are given at a plate boundary they indicate the vectors for the two adjacent plates. Thus, on the equator at 90° W, the Cocos Plate is spreading northeast and the Nazca Plate to the east.

These 'approved' hot spots (marked as red dots on Figure 3.3) include those beneath the Hawaiian islands and Iceland, and it is interesting that the Mid-Atlantic Ridge is thought to be migrating west across the Icelandic hot spot (cf. ITQ 3.1 for comment on migration further south in the Atlantic). Also shown in Figure 3.3 are absolute plate motion vectors, where the longest red arrows represent plate velocities of about 10 cm a^{-1} and the shortest 1 cm a^{-1}. A most striking feature of Figure 3.3 is that plate motions do not occur everywhere at right angles to plate boundaries. As you know, plate motions on a globe are best described in terms of *poles of rotation,* where the amount and direction of relative motion between two plates depends on the distance from the pole of rotation (see Figure 3.4). Now, the projection in Figure 3.3 greatly exaggerates high lines of latitude, but if you follow the vectors near the top of the map across the North American Plate (from Siberia to Alaska to Greenland) across the Atlantic Ridge (Iceland) to the European Plate (Poland) you can see that, very approximately, they describe the arc of a circle. On a globe, they would describe a *small circle* about a pole of rotation close to the Atlantic Ridge just north of the map boundary. With increasing distance from the pole, away to the south along the Atlantic Ridge, we find increased spreading rates, again consistent with spreading around small circles of increasing size (cf. Figure 3.4). Unfortunately, matters are not that simple everywhere, and, as you will see below, in an absolute frame of reference there need be no simple relationship of motion to plate boundaries.

The plate boundary processes with which we are all familiar — convergence and divergence — provide excellent descriptions of relative motion where this does occur at right angles to plate boundaries on the globe. Similarly, transverse (or strike–slip) motions parallel to conservative plate boundaries are easily understood. But there are many instances where oblique divergence, convergence or transform motion result in the combinations illustrated in Figures 3.5a and b. Plate boundaries where

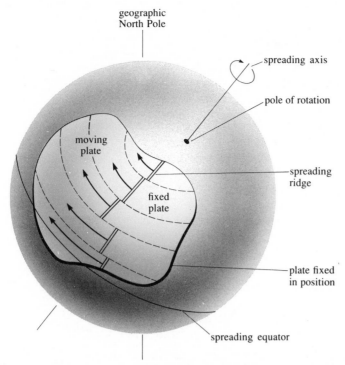

geographic
North Pole

spreading axis

pole of rotation

moving
plate

spreading
ridge

fixed
plate

plate fixed
in position

spreading equator

Figure 3.4 Diagram to illustrate how the motion of lithospheric plates can be described with reference to a pole of rotation. The dashed lines are small circles about a pole of relative plate rotation, and are parallel to the direction of movement of the plate. In this illustration, one plate is thought of as stationary while the other moves. Although the amount of opening is the same in terms of degrees all along the length of the spreading ridge, the spreading rate in centimetres per year increases away from the poles, as shown by the increasing lengths of the arrows, up to an angular distance of 90° — the spreading equator.

combinations of *transverse* and *compressional* motions occur are said to be undergoing **transpression**, whereas those combining *transverse* and *extensional* motions are undergoing **transtension**. Of course, few situations exist where relative motion is as simple as indicated in Figures 3.5a and b. Take the boundary between the Nazca and Cocos plates at 90° W on Figure 3.3, where the two vectors are given, and consider the relative motion in the *two* plates adjacent to this boundary.

Can you see any evidence for transpression or transtension here?

The Cocos vector points northeast, with motion at 45° to the Cocos–Nazca plate boundary, whereas the Nazca vector points just north of east, almost at right angles to the Nazca–Pacific plate boundary. So motion on the Nazca Plate side of the boundary in question is mainly strike–slip (parallel to the boundary), whereas that on the Cocos Plate is a combination of divergence and strike–slip, that is transtension. This is illustrated in Figure 3.5c. This type of transtensional boundary is also known as a **leaky transform fault** because normal strike–slip transform motions are combined with spreading and 'leakage' of magma. However, in this example, you will see that the strike–slip directions of motion are *not opposed* on either side of the boundary as you might expect from Figure 3.5b. This leads to another important feature of oceanic spreading, which is that transform faults that offset adjacent segments of ocean ridge (see, for example, Figures 3.1 and 3.3) may continue as prominent features across the ocean floor, particularly if there are differences in the style of spreading either side of the fault. In the case of the Cocos and Nazca Plates in Figures 3.3 and 3.5c, the strike–slip components of the overall motions are *both* towards the east, but there is an additional northwards-directed spreading component at right angles to the boundary in the Cocos Plate; thus the overall northeast motion in the Cocos Plate is a combination of the two components. To find the origin of the easterly-directed strike–slip motions, we must look further west (Figure 3.3), where we find the intersection between the Pacific Plate, Cocos Plate and Nazca Plate.

Figure 3.5 Combinations of convergence and divergence (black arrows) with strike–slip (half-headed arrows) leading to plate movement vectors (red arrows) at (a) a transpressional boundary, (b) a transtensional boundary, (c) the boundary between the Cocos and Nazca plates at 90° W, and (d) the boundary between the North American and Pacific plates at 130° W, 30° N. Plate boundaries are indicated by double lines with shading. Arrow lengths correspond to magnitudes of absolute plate velocities.

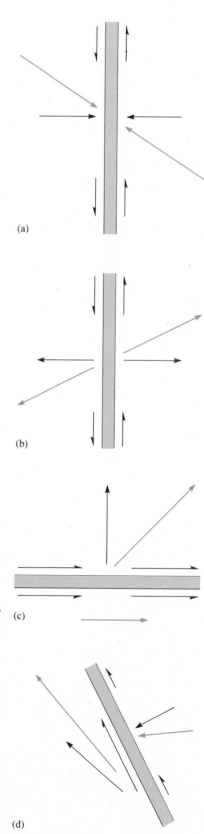

(a)

(b)

(c)

(d)

ITQ 3.2 (a) What do we call such an intersection between three plates?

(b) Can you now account for the origin of the strike–slip movement adjacent to the Cocos–Nazca boundary?

(c) How stable, or long-lasting, do you think this particular plate configuration will be as spreading continues?

Before continuing, it is important that you read our answer to ITQ 3.2, which is amplified below. There are several triple junctions between three ocean ridges (RRR triple junctions) shown in Figure 3.3, in the South Atlantic (*c*. 55° S, 0° W) and Indian Ocean (30° S, 65° E), for example. Because RRR are the only triple junctions that can persist with the same geometric configuration for several millions of years (see Figure 3.6a), they are also the commonest. Other types involving trenches (T) and transform faults (F) are unstable on geological time-scales, and, as you can see from Figures 3.6b and c, involve the movement of plate boundaries (in an absolute frame of reference) and rearrangements of their geometry. Returning to the Cocos–Nazca–Pacific plate triple junction, if it were behaving like the RRF junction shown in Figure 3.6c, then the strike–slip motion of the Nazca Plate with respect to the Cocos Plate would be to the west, opposite to the actual motion (Figures 3.3 and 3.5c). Moreover, the Cocos–Pacific boundary would, with time, become displaced to the east of the Nazca–Pacific boundary. We hope you can see, therefore, that this is behaving as a stable RRR triple junction, and, therefore, that the motions at the Cocos–Nazca boundary should also be stable. Notice, however, that there is shearing motion between the Caribbean and South American Plates further east, and that the latter will ultimately override the Nazca Plate while, all other motions being unchanged, the Cocos Plate will continue to grow.

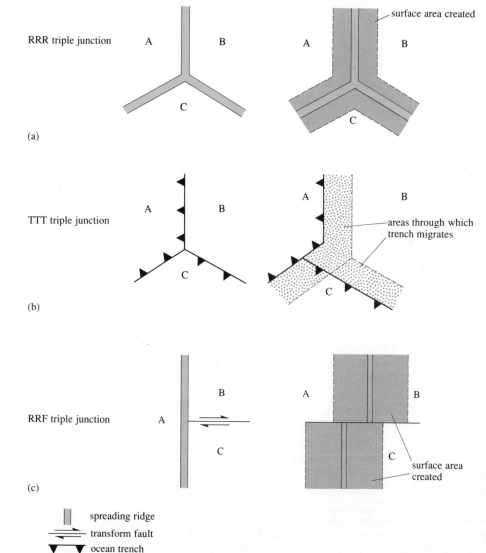

Figure 3.6 The evolution of triple junctions from left to right: (a) shows that an RRR triple junction is stable, and that the magnetic anomalies produced in the adjacent area will have Y-shaped patterns; (b) is a TTT junction, which may evolve in various ways depending on the location and extent of subduction; here it is assumed that no subduction occurs; TTT junctions are almost always unstable; (c) a junction between two ridges and a transform fault (RRF), which, again, can only exist for a short instant in geological time and is unstable because of the relative motion between plates B and C.

To complete this Section on the movement of plate boundaries, we need to consider one further example.

> What about the North American and Pacific plate boundary in California at 115° W, 30° N — what types of motion occur here? Is there transpression or transtension?

Here, the North American Plate, moving almost due west, is adjacent to the Pacific Plate which is spreading northwest at a much more rapid rate. Remember that Figure 3.3 shows absolute plate motions, and so the North American Plate must be overriding the Pacific Plate; there is obvious compression. The boundary between the two plates is a strike–slip boundary which runs the length of California: this may be familiar to you as the San Andreas Fault. So the North American–Pacific plate boundary involves convergence and minor strike–slip motion viewed from the American side and major strike–slip motion, at about 20° to the Pacific spreading vector, viewed from the Pacific side (Figure 3.5d). There is obviously major transpression adjacent to the boundary in the North American Plate and considerable transtension in the Pacific Plate. It is thought that the San Andreas fault system actually evolved from a transform fault off-setting adjacent segments of ocean ridge north and south of California. Clearly, *the plate boundary is actually moving west* with time, and so its geometric configuration is unstable.

The relative movements across the western American Plate boundary can best be illustrated by examining its history over the past 50 Ma, which is reconstructed in Figure 3.7. The evidence for this reconstruction comes from the analysis of magnetic anomaly patterns in the northeast Pacific, which tell us about the spreading history, combined with structural evidence for past and present tectonic processes in the North American Plate. Nevertheless, it is just one of several possible interpretations of the evidence, and you should bear this in mind as you read on. About 50 Ma ago, the Farallon Plate (a northerly continuation of the Cocos Plate in Figure 3.3) was spreading obliquely towards the North American Plate boundary where there was an active subduction zone. The ocean ridge separating the Pacific and Farallon Plates was segmented, with a series of transform offsets, as shown in Figure 3.7a. With time, the westerly movement of the North American Plate brought it into juxtaposition with the Pacific Plate, changing the boundary locally from one of convergence to one with strike–slip motion (Figure 3.7b). There is faster northwestwards strike–slip motion in the Pacific Plate than in the North American Plate because of the different magnitudes and directions of the plate motion vectors in the two adjacent plates. The embryonic San Andreas Fault in Figure 3.7b is almost, but not quite, parallel to the existing transform faults along the spreading ridge. The San Andreas Fault is often regarded as a transform fault itself. This process brought into being two triple junctions, the Mendocino triple junction to the north and the Rivera triple junction to the south. The present-day nature and configuration of these two triple junctions is illustrated in Figure 3.7c.

> What type(s) of triple junction are represented here?

The Mendocino triple junction is currently the point of intersection between a trench system to the north and two strike–slip faults; it is a TFF junction. The Rivera triple junction includes a ridge segment, a trench segment and a strike–slip fault and is an RTF junction. Both are geometrically unstable, and their nature has changed during the last 30 Ma as the North American Plate has advanced further over the ridge; at some times they are both RTF junctions and at others both TFF. The important point is that the new strike–slip fault has lengthened with time as the Farallon Plate has disappeared beneath North America, developing into the present-day San Andreas Fault at the expense of the subduction zone. The triple junctions have migrated apart along the North American–Pacific plate boundary, which itself has migrated west, eventually reaching the configuration illustrated in Figure 3.7c. Finally, you should note that this is a simplified picture; there is some evidence that early spreading in the Farallon Plate may have been to the northeast, which adds further complications that need not concern us here.

54

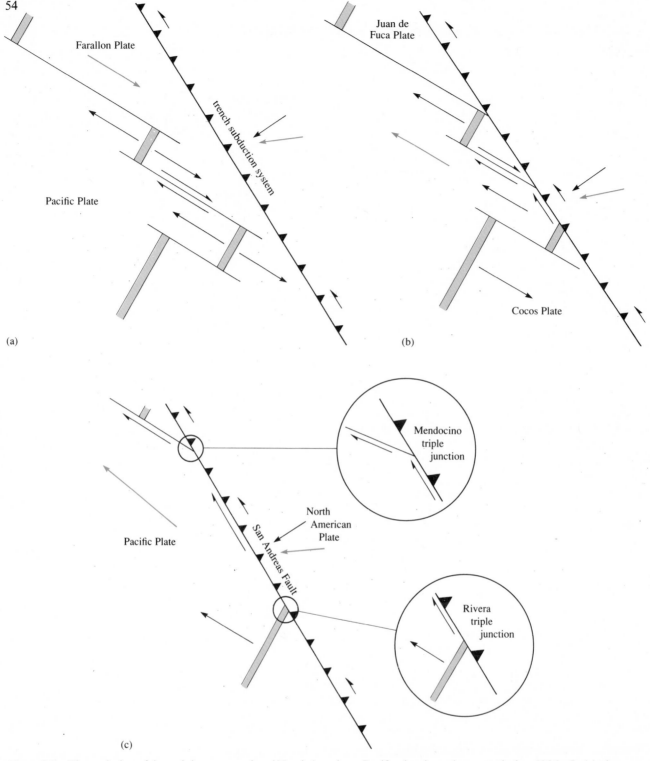

Figure 3.7 The evolution of the mainly transpressional North American–Pacific plate boundary over the last 50 Ma. In (a), the two are separated by the Farallon plate, which was being subducted beneath North America. 30 Ma ago in (b), triple junctions had formed where the Farallon plate had been overtaken and split into the Cocos and Juan de Fuca plates by N America migrating west. In (c), the present-day configuration, the two triple junctions have migrated apart as the transform San Andreas Fault system developed between adjacent segments of the Pacific–Farallon divergent plate boundary. Arrow lengths reflect magnitudes of absolute plate velocities.

Summary

What we have tried to demonstrate in this Section has been, quite simply, that plate boundaries are not permanent and fixed in an absolute frame of reference. Boundaries of all kinds may migrate according to the forces operating on them and this makes plate tectonics much more complicated than it might seem at first sight. Indeed, plate boundaries rarely lie exactly along a normal to small circles around the pole of rotation that determines plate movement (cf. Figure 3.4), and therefore they often involve mixtures of divergence and strike–slip (transtensive boundaries) or of compression and strike–slip (transpressive boundaries). Moreover, the character of boundaries may also change with time as they migrate into new stress regimes.

3.2 EXTENSIONAL PROCESSES ASSOCIATED WITH CONVERGENT BOUNDARIES

3.2.1 Extension at ocean–ocean convergent boundaries

Look again at Figure 3.3, this time at the western Pacific between Japan and Australia: the Philippine Plate. In terms of conventional, or simple views of plate tectonics, does anything strike you as odd about this area?

In an east–west cross-section from the Pacific Plate to the China Plate, there are two convergent boundaries with subduction zones. These are the Mariana arc to the east and the Ryukyu arc to the west — see Figure 3.8, which gives a tectonic analysis of the whole northwest Pacific area based on magnetic anomaly data. The Mariana and Ryukyu Ridges marked in this illustration are the two zones of island arc magmatism. As you can see, subduction is towards the west at both boundaries, but there are also divergent spreading axes *within* and behind the Philippine Plate. These include two extinct spreading axes in the Japan Sea to the north, the active Okinawa Trough behind the Ryukyu Ridge in the west, extinct spreading axes in the Shikoku and Parece-Vela Basins, also in the West Philippine Basin, and an active spreading axis in the Mariana Trough to the southeast of Figure 3.8. It should be clear from this illustration that some zones of oceanic lithospheric extension on the landward side of island arcs — in this case the Mariana and Okinawa spreading axes — are geometrically related in some way to the adjacent subduction zone.

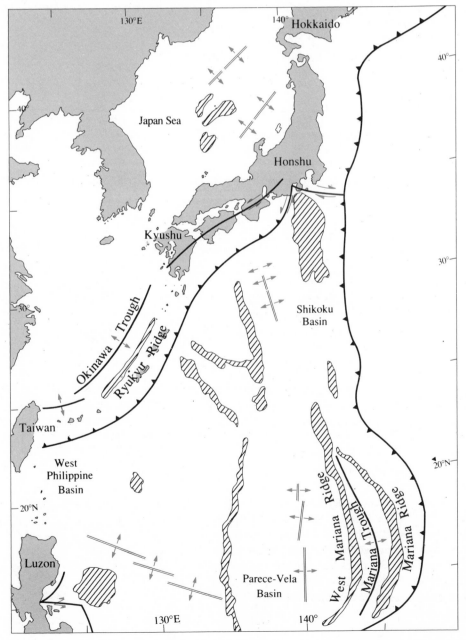

Figure 3.8 The back-arc basins of the northwestern Pacific, showing active spreading centres in continuous solid lines, extinct spreading centres in thin double lines and active trench systems in solid lines with 'teeth' to denote direction of subduction. Notice that in the Mariana area (bottom right) the island arc (easternmost ruled area) lies between the trench and Mariana trough back-arc spreading centre. The west Mariana Ridge and Parece–Vela spreading centre are a former arc and back-arc spreading system which was active 20 Ma ago.

These are by no means unique examples; similar spreading axes occur today in the Caribbean Sea and the Scotia Sea (Figure 3.3) behind the adjacent island arcs. The marginal position of small ocean basins such as the Philippine, Caribbean and Scotia Seas with respect to major ocean basins, in these cases the Pacific and the Atlantic, has led to them being called **marginal basins**. Because they are situated 'behind' (i.e. on the landward side of) island arcs, they are also sometimes known as **back-arc basins**. Here we shall use the term **back-arc spreading** to refer to extensional processes in marginal basins. You should note that the evidence from drilling and from seismic studies shows that the lithosphere in marginal basins has a structure broadly similar to that of larger ocean basins (i.e. sedimentary and basaltic layers overlying gabbroic crust and peridotite mantle). Moreover, the lithosphere associated with back-arc spreading axes seems to have very similar geophysical characteristics to that at ocean ridges.

What might be the cause of spreading behind the arc–trench systems of the western Pacific and Atlantic?

In each case, the *active* spreading zones (e.g. in the Mariana and Okinawa Troughs of Figure 3.8) lie some 100–200 km behind the main volcanic arc, which, itself, is *c*. 200 km from the trench. It follows that back-arc spreading axes may be related to the ascent of hot mantle material triggered in some way by the subduction process. The main melting processes, those that produced the island arc magmas, must have taken place some time before back-arc spreading magmas could be initiated. Of course, most of the volatiles that could promote melting in otherwise dry mantle will have been lost in arc magma generation. Moreover, the down-going plate is colder than the surrounding mantle, so it is difficult to see how large amounts of melt could be produced beneath back-arc spreading zones directly from subducted oceanic lithosphere. However, as we saw in Section 2.1.1 (Figures 2.9 and 2.10), only small thermal instabilities are needed for large amounts of shallow melting of suboceanic mantle to occur. An essential ingredient in the propagation of spreading processes at normal ocean ridges is the extensional stress regime, which causes adiabatic ascent of asthenosphere, hence partial melting.

Could there be similar tensional stresses across back-arc basins?

As you know from Figure 3.3, today some of the world's fastest spreading rates are associated with the Pacific, and, in the western Pacific, absolute convergence rates with Eurasia (specifically, the Chinese and Indian Plates) approach 10 cm a^{-1}. The western Pacific oceanic lithosphere is also old, approaching 200 Ma, and is therefore cold and dense; hence it is gravitationally unstable and is pulled down by the slab pull force (F_{SP}) well in front of the Chinese and Indian Plates, which are advancing from the west. Subduction is rapid, and this creates friction at the surface of the down-going plate. The important point is that *this friction induces convective processes in the asthenosphere*, affecting the lithosphere behind the trench, which, moreover, may also be under tension because a second trench system with its own slab-pull force is developing closer to the continental margin. The combined effects of this extensional stress regime and the possible thermal instabilities due to deep melting of the subducted plate provide the widely accepted explanation for back-arc spreading — see Figure 3.9. In these circumstances, it is probable that we can expect adiabatic ascent of asthenosphere material, as at ocean ridges (Figure 2.10), and partial melting due to near-surface decompression. Although the details of these processes are not yet fully understood, it is clear that back-arc spreading is best developed behind convergent boundaries with rapid closure; spreading rates are similar to those of the adjacent oceans, but most back-arc spreading basins have lifetimes of only *c*. 10 Ma.

Why should back-arc spreading centres have such a short life? (Think about what will happen as spreading continues at the back-arc axis in Figure 3.9.)

The main reason is that the spreading process itself forces the axis to migrate away from the adjacent arc (i.e. the spreading axis must move to the left in Figure 3.9). Looking again at Figure 3.8, if we regard the Mariana Trench (on the Pacific side of

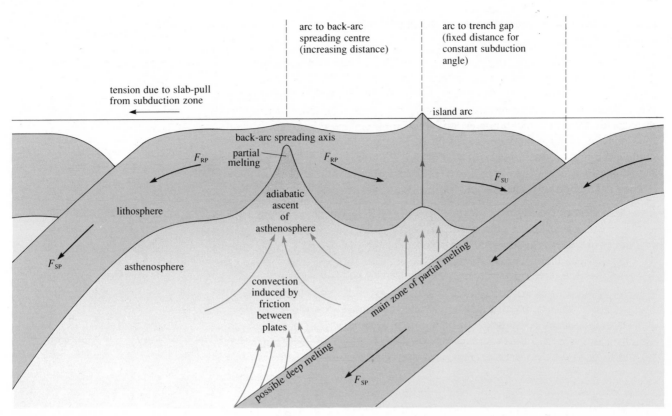

Figure 3.9 Simplified model for the development of spreading centres in back-arc marginal basins due to the combined effects of (i) friction-induced convection above the descending plate (see text), (ii) deep melting of the descending plate, and (iii) tension resulting from a second, landward subduction zone. These processes all promote adiabatic rise of asthenospheric material, followed by partial melting, as at normal ocean ridges. Forces are indicated following the terminology of Table 2.1.

the Mariana Ridge) as fixed, back-arc spreading at the Mariana Trough must be moving the whole of the West Mariana Ridge and Parece-Vela Basin to the west. Moreover, the Mariana Trough itself will move west but at half the rate of the Parece-Vela Basin, because spreading is taking place from the Mariana Trough towards the Mariana Ridge (i.e. the island arc). Eventually, the trough will move 'off-station' and no longer be located above the zone of friction-induced convection in the mantle (cf. Figure 3.9), and a new spreading axis will form further east, pushing the old one away west into the Philippine Sea. All these deductions follow from the assumption that the Mariana Trench is fixed in a hot-spot frame of reference, which is by no means certain, but they do serve to illustrate the reasons why back-arc spreading axes are short-lived in geological terms. It is not surprising, therefore, that several such extinct systems occur in marginal basins, and the Parece–Vela axis in Figure 3.8 probably was related to an earlier stage of the present overall tectonic regime. Clearly, however, the extinct spreading axis in the West Philippine Basin must relate to an earlier tectonic configuration, and it is the interpretation of detailed evidence of this type, preserved in complex marginal basins, that allows us to reconstruct the former tectonic history of continental margins.

One brief final point arises from our analysis of tectonics in the Philippine Sea. As you know from Figure 3.3, the China Plate is moving southeast in an absolute frame of reference and so will gradually encroach on the small-scale arc–trench systems of this marginal basin. The island arc parts of these systems will be of too low a density to be subducted, so during compression of the Philippine Sea, they may well be swept together to form a series of linear extinct volcanic arcs along the continental margin. This process of **island arc accretion** to continental margins has already occurred on the Pacific seaboard of Japan and is recorded frequently in plate-tectonic reconstructions of compressive events involving the closure of ocean basins bringing continents together (as illustrated schematically in Figure 2.27). We shall be illustrating and developing this theme more fully in Section 3.3 and again in Blocks 3 and 4.

3.2.2 Extension at ocean–continent convergent boundaries

In oceanic plate convergence zones, it seems that high closure rates are a critical factor in causing back-arc extensional spreading. But in addition to the magnitude of the plate closure vectors, it has also been suggested that the subduction angle is important in controlling the stress regime in the upper lithospheric slab, and that extensional stresses are greater over more steeply dipping subduction zones. On the eastern side of the Pacific, however, an important *continental* back-arc spreading zone appears to have been developed 30–40 Ma ago above the fast-moving but shallow-dipping subduction zone of the Farallon Plate (Figure 3.7). This is the **Basin and Range Province**, which is probably the best known example of a continental extensional regime developed behind a volcanic arc.

A modern view of the Basin and Range Province (BRP) is given in Figure 3.10. In northern California and, to the north, in Oregon and Washington State are the Cascades volcanoes (including Mt St Helens) associated with active subduction of the Juan de Fuca Plate. The BRP extends 1 000 km across California, Nevada and into Utah. It narrows to the south and bends around the Colorado Plateau (a zone of isostatic uplift) to link with the north–south Rio Grande rift of New Mexico. It consists of an elongate, parallel ridge-and-valley topography controlled by normal (extensional) faults in response to the minimum horizontal stress (maximum extension) direction which, today, averages WNW–ESE (Figure 3.10). The range blocks are about 25–35 km from crest to crest, with intervening basins 10–20 km wide.

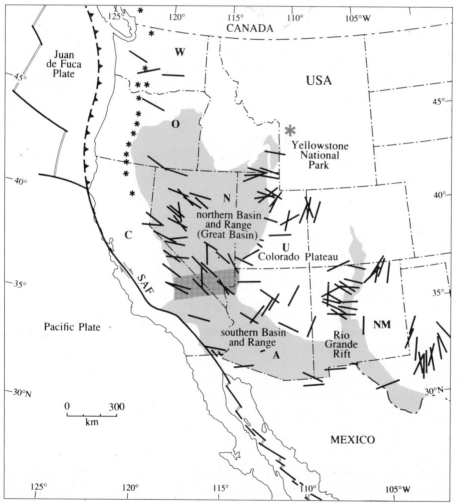

Figure 3.10 Location of the Basin and Range extensional province (BRP) in relation to the current plate boundary between the American and Pacific plates (from north to south, the Juan de Fuca plate subduction zone with Cascades volcanoes marked by asterisks, the San Andreas transform fault, SAF, and the Cocos–Pacific ridge transform system of the Gulf of California). The grey region across southern California and Nevada is the boundary zone between the northern and southern Basin and Range (details in text). The short black lines represent current directions of *least* principal horizontal stress, parallel to maximum extension, as derived from earthquake focal mechanisms, *in situ* stress measurements and a variety of geological data. Throughout most of the BRP, these indicate extension in a WNW–ESE direction (dot–dash lines are state boundaries; C, California; O, Oregon; W, Washington State; N, Nevada; U, Utah; A, Arizona; NM, New Mexico).

This would be a particularly appropriate point to consolidate your understanding by watching the first 10 minutes of *Extensional Tectonics*, the first track on video-cassette VC 271. This explains the background to the tectonic evolution of the BRP; you should return to this text at the point where the first graphics of listric fault structures appear in the programme. (You need not worry too much if it is inconvenient to view the programme now, but you will need to do so at the end of this Section).

Briefly, the programme explains that following the late Mesozoic compression and associated igneous intrusive events that built the Sierra Nevada and Rocky Mountains of NW America, there has been intermittent extension during the last 40 Ma, and particularly during the last 25 Ma. Across the BRP today, we have high continental heat flow (Figure 2.26), a regional Bouguer gravity low (indicating lower than average densities beneath the province), and low seismic velocities in the upper mantle. This evidence combines to indicate that the BRP is a region of thin lithosphere, shallow asthenosphere and hot, low density material, which, intermittently, is partially molten at shallow depth. Indeed, there is still abundant evidence of contemporary igneous activity on the northern edge of the BRP at Yellowstone (Figure 3.10), and volcanism within the province during the last 30 Ma has produced widespread, originally horizontal, basalt lava flows (further details below). Regional variation in remanent magnetism in some of the older basalts indicates that a total of about 50 km extension has occurred across the BRP in the last 25 Ma. As you know from Figure 3.7 and Section 3.1, during this time the character of the ocean–continent convergence zone west of the BRP has been changing. The evolution of the BRP is intimately connected with this change in character as you will see from the analysis that we develop below.

Data on volcanic feeder dykes and fault slips suggest that the *modern* extensional regime in Figure 3.10 was superimposed on the effects of an older extensional regime and that the modern regime developed earlier (*c*. 13 Ma ago) in the south than in the north (*c*. 10 Ma ago). In particular, the orientation of the stress field appears to have changed with the development of the modern structure of the southern BRP in the last 13 Ma. This, combined with the change in extension direction from the north to south of the BRP (Figure 3.10), and the fact that the south is now seismically quiet compared with the north, has led to the distinction between the northern and the southern BRP.

Overall, extension *preceding* the formation within the region of the modern basin and range topography apparently was well underway by 30 Ma ago but peaked in the period 10–20 Ma ago, as inferred from (i) the presence of folded and highly tilted strata exposed in recent range blocks, (ii) stratigraphic data on the thickness and distribution of basinal sedimentary units, and (iii) the abundant extension-related basaltic magmatism starting in the south 30 Ma ago and extending to the north by 17 Ma ago.

> **ITQ 3.3** (a) What does the presence of erupted basalt magma suggest about the magnitude of β, the stretch factor, and the heat flow during extension?
>
> (b) Locally, about 15 Ma ago, extensions of 50–100% apparently were developed in about 1 Ma during this early stage of BRP extension; what strain rates must have been operating, and is this consistent with your answer to (a)?

Notice that extensions of 50–100% are identical to stretch factors (β) of 1.5–2.0, the value we gave for the BRP at the end of Section 2.2.3. Heat flow even today in the BRP is $90 \, \text{mW m}^{-2}$ compared with $60 \, \text{mW m}^{-2}$ on the flanks (Figure 2.26), and would probably have been even greater 20 Ma ago, allowing strain softening to occur. Of course, strain rates of $10^{-14} \, \text{s}^{-1}$ and greater did not continue, or an ocean basin would have formed during the last 15 Ma. In fact, strain rates have now decreased to $5 \times 10^{-15} \, \text{s}^{-1}$, so extensional deformation has definitely slowed down, despite the continuing high heat flow.

> Can you suggest in terms of plate motions why strain rates might have decreased; how much further will the BRP develop if there is no increase in strain rate?

The answer to this question takes us back to Figure 3.7 and the evolution of the America–Pacific plate boundary. Active subduction to the west ceased along the Californian coast during the period since 30 Ma ago, and this will have reduced both the convectional stresses induced by friction and any input of magma from deep levels. So the cessation of subduction and the slowing of strain rates seem to be linked in time suggesting that the mechanism of back-arc 'spreading' in continents is similar to that of oceans (Figure 3.9). *Spreading in the BRP has slowed, on this model, because subduction no longer occurs and the associated stresses have reduced.* A slowing of the extension rate will lead to *strain hardening* (Figures 2.29 and 2.30) and eventually the BRP system will become locked.

The relationship between the plate boundary stress field and the style/timing of tectonism in the BRP has been studied by Mary Lou Zoback and co-workers from the US Geological Survey. They have drawn attention to the fact that the *early* extensional structures tend to be orientated ENE–WSW, parallel to the former direction of compression (black arrows in Figure 3.11). *Later* structures were developed in the modern WNW–ESE extensional stress field (red arrows in Figure 3.11, see also Figure 3.10). According to Zoback, this reorientation was directly related to the development of the San Andreas Fault, which has a strong component of northwards shear in an absolute frame of reference (Figure 3.7). Indeed (cf. Figure 3.11), 10–20 Ma ago, the presence of back-arc spreading behind the subduction boundary would have created ENE–WSW extensional stress. Today, following the northwards migration of the Mendocino triple junction, the same extensional stresses exist, but only from further north. *The progressive clockwise rotation of extensional strain axes has therefore been attributed to the progressive northwards migration of the southern end of the subduction zone, as indicated in Figure 3.11.*

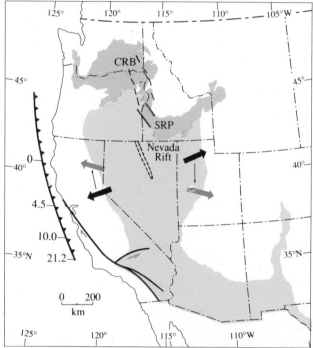

Figure 3.11 Clockwise change in the least principal stress direction *c*. 10 Ma ago in the Basin and Range province due to progressive change from subduction to transform tectonics along the America–Pacific plate boundary. Numbers along the subduction zone show the southern extent of subduction in Ma as the Mendocino triple junction migrated north. Heavy black arrows give least principal stress direction prior to *c*. 10 Ma ago; red arrows indicate current direction. CRB and SRP show the limits of the Columbia River Plateau basalts and those of the Snake River Plain, both associated with a NNW-trending zone of rifting.

Another important feature of extensional tectonics in the northern BRP is the presence of a 300 km long NNW-trending rift zone in northern Nevada (the Nevada Rift), together with a similar, but wider graben at the western end of the Snake River Plain (SRP) which continues north beneath the Columbia River (CRB) area. These are zones of intense dyking, feeding the *vast* area of lavas shown in Figure 3.11, which contain nearly 2×10^5 km^3 of extensional 'flood' basalts with ages between 14 and 17 Ma. This is a huge volume of basalt by any standards and represents a productivity rather higher than the typical eruption rate of a fast-spreading ocean ridge. Clearly, if the Pacific–Farallon plate boundary had not been consumed beneath California, and had the early BRP stress regime continued, the whole of continental north America would have been split, with a new ocean forming some 500 km east of the present west coast!

Finally, we need to consider the tectonic behaviour of the whole continental lithosphere beneath the BRP rather than just the surface features discussed so far. Zoback and co-workers believe that in the main deformation phase, when there were high strain rates about 15 Ma ago, brittle normal faulting affected the whole of the upper crust, down to a depth of 15 km. In this area, the crust consists of 1 400 Ma old quartz-rich gneisses.

Is 15 km a plausible depth for brittle failure to penetrate in a quartz-dominated rheology?

Figure 2.23b shows that the brittle zone can reach 10 km depth at a heat flow of $90 \, mW \, m^{-2}$, but normal faults would be unlikely to penetrate to greater depths simply as *brittle* structures. However, it is possible, though much debated, that they traverse a ductile zone to connect with deeper (lower crust and upper mantle) low-angle (0–30°) faults that could represent major detachment zones penetrating through the ductile layer and affecting the whole lithosphere. There is some evidence for such deep structural detachments from reflection seismology, for example around coastal Britain — see Block 1B; for the moment, we need to consider the implications of these hypothesized deep low-angle structures. Their significance is that they provide important information on the nature and mechanisms of lithospheric extension processes, as you will find below, and in two video sequences at the end of this Section.

First, are low-angle structures consistent with the uniform stretching model of basin formation advocated by Dan McKenzie which tends to produce symmetrical structures as illustrated in Figure 2.15?

The McKenzie model requires that the crust and mantle lithosphere are attenuated uniformly along any given vertical reference line (see also Figure 2.29), so that detachments due to relative movements within the ductile zone beneath the basin will not occur. This is known as a **pure shear model**, and it is usually taken to involve symmetrical brittle normal faulting above the brittle–ductile transition zone (Figure 3.12a) and symmetrical extension by ductile flow below this transition. In pure shear, the whole lithosphere behaves homogeneously and is drawn out like a piece of toffee. So the answer to the question above is that deep low-angle detachment zones are *not* a feature of McKenzie's stretching model.

To accommodate these deep detachment zones, Brian Wernicke of Harvard University has proposed an alternative model of basin formation. This model involves **simple shear**, which requires that the thickness of a sheared block, measured at right angles to the planes of movement, remains unchanged. If you look at Wernicke's model for the upper crust in Figure 3.12c, for example, each parallel-sided block remains unchanged in thickness, but the overall effect of movement concentrated on the planes between is that the crust is thinned in a vertical sense. Don't worry if you find this a bit difficult to envisage as it is illustrated in the video programmes at the end of this Section. The really important thing to notice is that *in Wernicke's model, relative extension of the lithosphere is asymmetrical, and along any vertical line the amount of extension in the crust and mantle is non-uniform* (Figure 3.12c). This is because there are large detachments connecting the near-surface zone of normal faulting with the deep asthenospheric extension zone, which is therefore laterally offset from the zone of crustal extension. Notice that the deep low-angle detachment zone is a concave upwards fault that flattens at depth — known as a **listric fault** (Figure 3.13) — which changes from near vertical to the left and becomes progressively more shallow to the right with increasing depth (cf. Figure 3.13). Figure 3.13 illustrates the mechanics of listric faulting in which simple lateral displacements at depth would produce a gap in the crust at the surface. This is a gravitationally unstable situation, so crust in the hanging-wall block (the block *above* the fault surface) bends and rotates to form an anticlinal structure, known as a **roll-over**. The volume vacated by the roll-over (A) will be the same as that created by extension (B). More commonly, the roll-over zone undergoes brittle fracture, producing blocks that are carried along the fault surface in a so-called **breakaway zone**.

Indeed a notable feature of the BRP core is the presence of blocks with consistent tilt directions, towards the west, and this suggests that extension has been accomplished mainly by individual brittle faulted blocks being carried east along a low-angle detachment. In an amplified and extended view of the model of lithospheric extension by simple shear, Figure 3.14, this appears as an extensive upper crustal breakaway zone. It is in this zone (zone B) that the major topographic depression

62

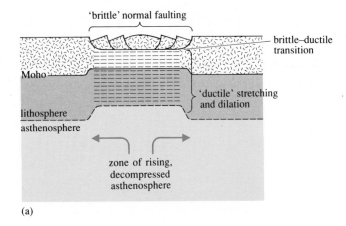

(a)

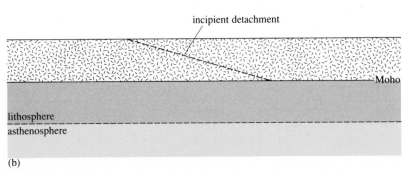

(b)

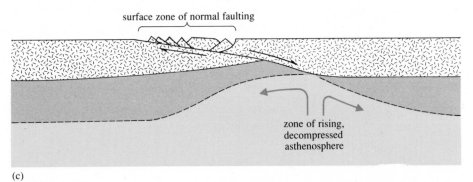

(c)

Figure 3.12   Illustration of the two end-member models for lithospheric extension and basin formation. (a) Shows the McKenzie model, involving pure shear, which was developed in Section 2.2.3; deformation in both brittle and ductile layers is uniform. (b) and (c) are successive stages in the Wernicke model, involving simple shear, where brittle fault blocks are carried along a shear plane that propogates through the entire lithosphere; deformation in both brittle and ductile layers is asymmetrical.

occurs, because this is a zone of net crustal thinning, so that sedimentation may start to fill the basin during extension. In the case of the Basin and Range Province, sedimentation rates have been low so the deep structures remain unburied. Notice that in the model, the listric fault surface, which is a zone of detachment between the upper and lower blocks penetrates the mantle lithosphere further to the right. This **detachment zone** is seen at the surface, together with the most uplifted rocks from the deepest crust — often termed a **core complex** — in Figure 3.14 just left of where the crust is thinnest (i.e. right of zone B). Notice that in zone B the crust has extended but the mantle lithosphere has not. There is **tectonic subsidence** because of stretching in the crust and also some later thermal subsidence because the whole lithosphere section was thinned by crustal extension, and so asthenosphere at the base must thermally relax after extension stops, forming new lithosphere — a process involving some contraction.

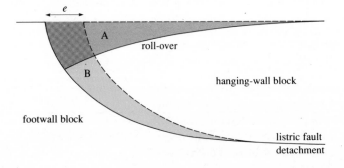

Figure 3.13   A simple listric normal (tensional) fault — solid line — and associated near-surface roll-over. The dashed line shows the upper, hanging-wall block as it will appear after horizontal extension e at the surface in the absence of gravity. This would produce a gap in the section (B — red area). As the hanging-wall rolls over during faulting, its shape is controlled by conservation of volume, expressed by the grey area (A) being equal to the red area (B).

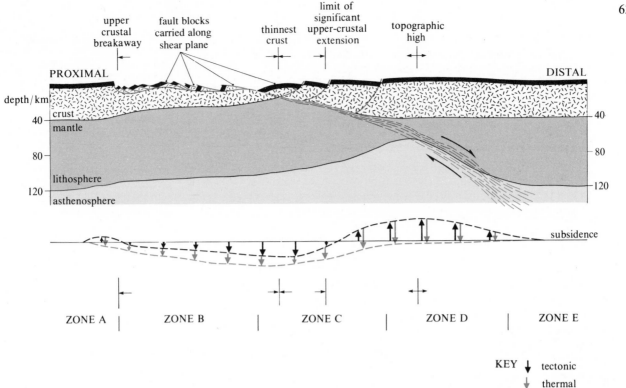

Figure 3.14 Detailed illustration of the Wernicke model for extensional basin development as applied to the Basin and Range province (see text for detailed tectonic description). There is no extension in zones A and E, though tectonic rebound and thermal subsidence from adjacent areas may develop. In zone B, the brittle crustal zone is extended but not the ductile mantle layer. In zone C, both extension and subsidence reach a maximum; in zone D, there is extension only in the sheared ductile mantle layer.

In zone C, there are large normally faulted blocks dipping in the opposite direction and each sitting on a listric fault surface. The zone of maximum crustal attenuation and hence maximum net tectonic subsidence is at the left of zone C. A change from tectonic subsidence to **tectonic uplift** occurs further to the right because, here, the effect of mantle thinning becomes more important than crustal thinning and the consequent ascent of asthenosphere creates initial uplift.

> However, thermal subsidence after extension has ceased also increases to the right. Why is this?

This is because, once the hot asthenosphere cools back to normal temperatures, causing the mantle lithosphere to return to its original thickness, the associated contraction effect largely compensates for the initial tectonic uplift. In fact, right across Figure 3.14, *overall* subsidence occurs only where the brittle upper lithosphere zone (the low density crust) is thinned. In zone D, where there is only thinning of the mantle lithosphere (the crust is not involved), the initial tectonic uplift is almost exactly cancelled by the later thermal subsidence. Here, however, erosion of the initial dome may effectively thin the crust, thereby causing the thermal subsidence to exceed initial uplift. Finally, both zones A and E are not affected by the extensional regime.

> Where, according to the Wernicke model, do you think basalt magmas are most likely to invade the extended lithosphere?

If we allow the extensional situation to develop further than shown in Figure 3.14, the brittle zone will continue to thin in zone C; on the other hand, mantle asthenosphere is rising beneath zone D. So the net result is that magmas might invade the crust first near the boundary between zones C and D, well to the distal side of the main basin. Indeed, the whole basis of Wernicke's model for basin formation is that it is markedly asymmetrical with the position of thinning in the uppermost brittle extension zone not above that in the ductile lithosphere beneath. As you can see from Figure 3.14, this has consequences for the style of block faulting in the upper crust and for uplift and subsidence rates that can be tested by observation.

Pure and simple shear models for extensional basin formation have been developed for several different continental basins, including the Basin and Range Province and the North Sea. Although there is considerable debate about how widely applicable each model may be, the Wernicke simple shear model clearly has some relevance to the evolution of the BRP. It is quite possible that the two models may relate to the differing tectonic situations in which basins are developed, though clear links to active rift zones (with upwelling asthenospheric convection) and to passive rift zones (due to regional extensional stresses) have not yet been developed. In the case of the BRP, extension is thought to reflect back-arc spreading processes beneath the lithosphere, with upwelling asthenosphere, particularly on the western (proximal in Figure 3.14) side of the extension zone. Nevertheless, there are those who prefer to think of the BRP as a passive rift, merely reflecting the regional tectonic stress regime.

You will meet these models for basin formation again in Block 2, when we consider the evolution of rift zones in the Midland Valley of Scotland and in the Red Sea. Meanwhile, to consolidate your understanding of this Section, and particularly the debate about the two models, you should now view the two programmes on extensional processes on videocassette VC 271: *Extensional Tectonics*, and *Extension in the North Sea*. The first programme looks at some of the field evidence for the processes of extension and tectonic faulting in the BRP, developing both the Wernicke model in graphic form and discussing the influence of the overall Mesozoic–Tertiary tectonic evolution of western North America. It will therefore help you to revise aspects of both Section 3.1 (Figure 3.7) and 3.2 (Figure 3.14). The second programme concentrates on the McKenzie model, and is thus relevant to parts of Section 2.1.2 (Figure 2.15) as well as Section 3.2. It describes some of the seismic and thermal data from the North Sea area that relate to extension, first during the Permo-Triassic period, and then again more recently. You need not worry about the fine detail of seismic reflection data as we shall be introducing the information required in this Course in Block 1B, and also in Block 5. The two programmes take 23 and 30 minutes; you should view them now, and then attempt the following ITQs.

ITQ 3.4   According to the video programme *Extensional Tectonics*:

(a) What geological feature forms the western limit of the province undergoing extension?

(b) What geological horizon forms the most useful marker for assessing the effect on extension of vertical movements and block rotation?

(c) What rocks are exposed in the core complex and how deeply have they been buried in the crust?

(d) Is the BRP an active or a passive rift?

ITQ 3.5   According to the video programme *Extension in the North Sea*:

(a) What has detailed analysis of sedimentary logs by McKenzie's group, coupled with seismic interpretation, revealed about the extension history of the Central Graben of the North Sea?

(b) What is the essential contrast in the zone of highest heat flow during extension on the McKenzie and the Wernicke basin extension models?

(c) Which model is preferred on the basis of seismic data from the UK–Norwegian sector, and what two inferred structural features most strongly support this model?

Summary

In Section 3.2, we have considered the extensional processes that affect the lithosphere behind convergent plate boundaries where spreading rates are high and, perhaps, subduction angles are steep.

1   The principal cause of tensional stress (Figure 3.9) may be due to frictional coupling between the down-going plate and adjacent, overlying asthenosphere.

Back-arc spreading in the marginal basins of oceanic areas occurs as deep magmas from the subducting slab, combined with much more extensive partial melts from the overlying mantle, rise to form spreading axes that are generally short lived, because they must necessarily migrate from the adjacent arc.

2   The same processes can affect continental lithosphere, and we have examined the tectonic history of the Basin and Range Province (western USA) in some detail, noting that two phases of extension (before and after *c*. 13 Ma) are apparently related to changes in the stress regime due to the progressive evolution from subduction to transform movements at the western American Plate boundary (Figure 3.11).

3   Following the pure shear (symmetrical) model of basin formation, introduced earlier — the McKenzie model (Figure 2.15) — we have developed a second, simple shear asymmetrical model (Figure 3.14) that seems to account well for pre-13 Ma extension in the BRP. This involves whole lithosphere faulting with major detachment shear zones developing through the ductile lithosphere. These detachments carry and rotate individual normal fault blocks on listric fault surfaces within the brittle upper lithosphere. This has become known as the Wernicke model. While the McKenzie model seems to provide a good explanation for extension in the Central Graben of the North Sea, there is more debate about the origin of the Viking Graben, further north, and there is some evidence favouring the application of the Wernicke model to this area.

3.3   CONTINENTAL EVOLUTION BY TERRANE ACCRETION

Plate tectonic processes are responsible for the *formation of* continental crust at destructive plate margins. For example, at active margins, such as around the Pacific Ocean, continents grow in volume by addition of igneous material from the mantle below and by the build-up of accretionary prisms between the oceanic trenches and the continental margin. The area of continental crust may be further extended at passive margins such as around the Atlantic Ocean by the build-up of river-borne clastic sediments and carbonates along the coastal margin. But have you ever stopped to think about what happens where strike–slip motions characterize continental margins?

> Consider coastal California, for example, (cf. Figure 3.3). From what you know of motions at the North American–Pacific Plate boundary (Figure 3.7), how is coastal California moving relative to North America?

Strike–slip motions along the ever-lengthening San Andreas Fault are carrying coastal California northwards relative to North America, at an overall rate of several centimetres a year. This has led to the rather delightful forecast that Los Angeles (SW California) will have become a new suburb of San Francisco (N California) a mere 30 Ma into the future (see Figure 3.15). Clearly, we have defined a fragment of continental lithosphere that is moving independently with respect to the adjacent main body of continental North America, and that, ultimately, will be displaced far to the north of its original location. This example is by no means unique, so that a major process of continental evolution involves the rearrangement and welding of continental blocks (including island arcs) known as **terranes** to a pre-existing continental margin.

But what exactly do we mean by the word terrane? The following definition is taken from David Howell's article 'Terranes' in *Scientific American,* November 1985:

> 'In geology the word terrain simply designates the lay of the land. In contrast, the term terrane (the full name is tectonostratigraphic terrane) designates a crustal block, not necessarily of uniform composition, bounded by faults. It is a geologic entity whose history is distinct from the histories of adjoining terranes. Terranes come in many sizes and shapes, and they have varying degrees of compositional complexity. India, for example, is a single great terrane. Some of its individual rock formations have ages exceeding a billion years; conversely, the terranes that did not originate as a fragment of some earlier continent generally embody a fairly simple history spanning less than 200 million years, the normal maximum survival time for an ocean floor.'

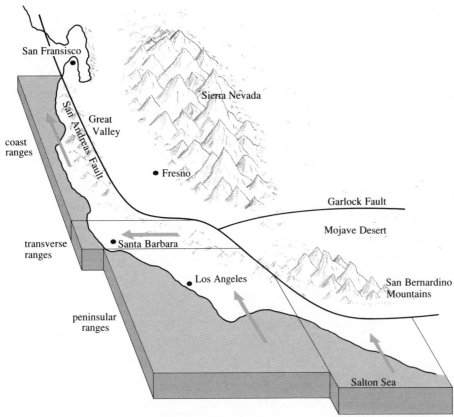

Figure 3.15 A simplified map of the San Andreas Fault system in California, showing the general northwards movement of lithospheric blocks along the west coast of North America. Note that the cities of Los Angeles and Santa Barbara lie on these mobile blocks whereas San Francisco lies just to the east, on the North American Plate.

This last comment refers to the possibility that any terrane (such as coastal California) may exist and move independently so long as the ocean that provided the tectonic stresses to mobilize it as a discrete block is able to survive. For example, looking into the distant future, imagine what would happen were the northern Pacific to close in *c*. 80 Ma by subduction beneath Asia, allowing 8 000 km of ocean to be closed at a net convergence rate of 10 cm a^{-1}. Both the island arc terranes of the NW Pacific, which were born within the oceanic plate, and the continental terranes of North America may become welded into a new continent. You will not be surprised that terrane geometry, i.e. the shape of terrane blocks, is exceedingly variable. To quote from the same article:

> 'The geometry of a terrane is the product of its history of movements and tectonic interactions. Terranes born on an oceanic plate retain their shape until they collide and accrete. Then they are subject to crustal movements that modify their shape. For example, the terranes of the Brooks Range in Alaska (part of the compressional mountain belt) are great sheets stacked one on top of another. Elsewhere in the cordillera, or chain of mountain ranges, in western North America the terranes are elongated bodies. The elongation reflects the slicing of the crust by a network of north-west-trending faults including the San Andreas fault of California. In Asia the terranes tend to have retained the shapes they inherited from episodes of rifting; some smaller terranes, however, were caught in collisions between the larger ones and got distorted. The assemblage of terranes in China is being stretched and displaced in east–west directions as India continues to squeeze Asia from the south.'

The terranes within China and Asia to which Howell is referring here are now caught up *within* a continent and the processes involved will be discussed in Blocks 4 and 6. Not surprisingly, their recognition both in modern and ancient collision zones is now revolutionizing our interpretation of geological and tectonic events in the past, not least in terms of the widely scattered locations from which the different fragments now assembled into single continents have come. Howell continues:

> 'The precise history of the movement of an individual terrane is not always known. Indeed, it is only recently that paths have been documented for a few of the Earth's

terranes. Since by definition terranes are fault-bounded and distinct from their geologic surroundings, each of them must have moved a distance at least equal to its longest dimension. The actual distances vary greatly. Some basaltic seamounts now accreted to the margin of Oregon have moved a minimal distance, from a nearby offshore origin. Yet similar rock formations around San Francisco have come as far as 4 000 kilometers across the Pacific. At a rate of just 10 centimetres per year a wandering terrane could complete a circuit of the globe in just 400 million years. Little wonder that the continents are patchwork agglomerations of terranes.'

It is a sobering thought, especially given that motions of lithospheric plates could well have been much faster in geological past, that the continental masses so familiar to us today may be the result of such large-scale and long distance motions between much smaller 'jig-saw pieces' in the past.

You are probably wondering how such large and rapid motions can occur within the framework of plate vectors as we know them. Take the example of India, a single large terrane block recently welded to continental Asia. Figure 3.16 gives a tectonic reconstruction of the Indian Ocean 75 and 35 Ma ago during the spreading apart of the southern continents at which time a large ocean — Tethys — occupied the vast open area between the southern continents.

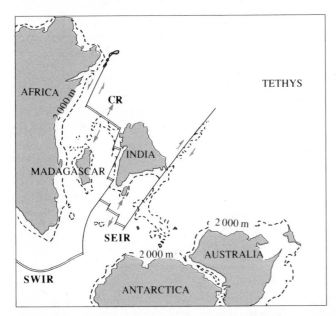
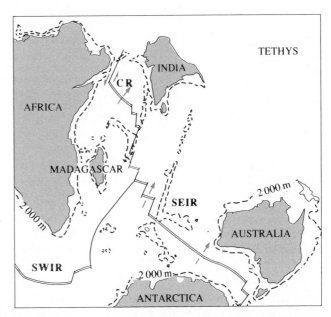

Figure 3.16   (a) The relative positions of spreading axes, transform faults, and the major present-day continental land masses in the Indian Ocean as they are believed to have been 75 Ma ago. Arrows show the directions of relative movement of plates. (Broken outline is the 2 000 m contour below sea-level.) (b) The relative positions of spreading axes, transform faults, and the major present-day continental land masses in the Indian Ocean as they are believed to have been 35 Ma ago. (CR, Carlsberg Ridge; SEIR, Southeast Indian Ridge; SWIR, Southwest Indian Ridge; TETHYS, former ocean that closed when India collided with Asia — further details in text.)

ITQ 3.6   Using Figure 3.16, can you explain the rapid northeast migration of India during the 75–35 Ma time interval:

(a) in terms of the role of spreading ridges and transform faults?

(b) in terms of likely sources of stress causing this migration?

This type of analysis has shown that India moved about 6 600 km in total, over 80 Ma, an average rate of motion of 8 cm a^{-1}, and this comprises both the half-spreading rate of the Carlsberg–Southeast Indian Ridge system and its northeastwards migration relative to Africa. (Note that we cannot be sure that this is absolute motion, but palaeomagnetic data from India suggest that most of this 6 600 km movement has been towards the north.) There really is nothing exceptional about this example, except perhaps that it involves rather a large terrane block moving rather more rapidly than usual. What it does illustrate very clearly is that when a continental extension zone develops into an ocean ridge, newly detached terrane blocks can then be moved large distances at right angles to the new spreading ridge — in fact parallel to small circles around the pole of rotation represented by transform faults.

To appreciate the size and complexity of terrane accretion processes, we return to the western North American cordilleran belt, discussed by Howell, where the concept of **displaced terranes** was first developed by David Jones, Peter Coney and co-workers at the US Geological Survey and University of Arizona. These displaced terranes are sometimes called 'exotic' because of their geological contrast with the adjacent continent, and, in cases where there is doubt about their origin, they are sometimes called 'suspect' terranes. Here, we will stick to the term displaced terrane. Jones and Coney made the point that although displaced terranes of the type we have been discussing may be found at any convergent boundary, and are therefore prominent in the central Asian collision zone where India eventually collided with Asia (see Block 6), they are particularly associated with strike–slip regimes. They tend to accumulate in geometrically favourable locations, along boundaries where there is prominent transpression. Figure 3.17 illustrates the immense complexity of the North American Pacific seaboard, over 70% of which is made up of discrete terranes.

The techniques used to identify the individual terranes shown in Figure 3.17 were first, *abrupt discontinuities* in rock sequences across major faults, implying very different geological histories in terranes that are now adjacent. Second, similar discontinuities in the *fossil record* were employed; for example, tropical fossil forms in displaced terranes are easily distinguished from the cool–temperate forms expected at these latitudes. Third, the displaced terranes exhibit markedly different *palaeomagnetic characteristics,* which, in some cases, allow possible source locations to be identified. Most of the terranes of coastal North America appear to have collided and accreted to the craton margin during Mesozoic and early Cenozoic time. Many show evidence of an origin far distant from their present position, and may have moved hundreds of kilometres after accretion. Palaeomagnetic evidence also indicates significant rotations about the vertical in many cases. It appears that strike–slip motions on the Pacific borders with North America have been perpetuated throughout the last 100–120 Ma and that many terranes may have originated on the far side of the Pacific; some of the evidence is presented below.

One of the first terranes to be identified was the *Cache Creek terrane*, which occurs 300 km inland in western Canada (Figure 3.17). The Cache Creek rocks consist of thick sequences of late Palaeozoic shallow-water limestones deposited directly onto mafic and ultramafic crust. Adjacent, and on the Pacific side, is the *Stikine terrane,* which comprises Permian to middle Jurassic acid to basic volcanic layers within similar volcanogenic sediments all showing extensive thrusting, especially in the north. This is followed by the *Tracy Arm terrane,* with a complex assemblage of high-grade continental origin metamorphic schists and gneisses of unknown age.

> Would you say that the rocks are becoming more oceanic or more continental from east to west?

This particular sequence of terranes seems to be more continental in affinity *towards* the coast, with marine limestones resting on probable oceanic crust within the most easterly Cache Creek terrane. There is no clear east–west age trend, though the youngest Upper Mesozoic–Cenozoic rocks do occur in the *Chugach terrane,* right on the Pacific coast of the Canada–Alaska border. Here, in the top northeast corner of the Pacific, thrusting of terranes seems to have been more prevalent than strike–slip motions, probably because the strong transform movements further south have yet to reach this zone (Figure 3.7).

Returning to the Cache Creek terrane, the marine sediments contain certain distinctive marine protozoan microfossils known as *fusulinids.* These are a particularly large (up to 4 cm) genus of the normally microscopic Foraminifera, and date back to the Permian. One specific type of fusulinid is widely distributed in the older terranes of westernmost America, but is totally unlike the species found further east in the Rocky Mountains (Figure 3.18). The forms present in the Cache Creek and other terranes belong to the species widely distributed through China, Japan, the East Indies and the Malay Peninsula. Indeed, these Asian fusulinids help to define a **Tethyan faunal province**, a term that alludes again to the ancient Tethyan ocean that, in Permian times, lay to the south-east of the Eurasian continent and that closed

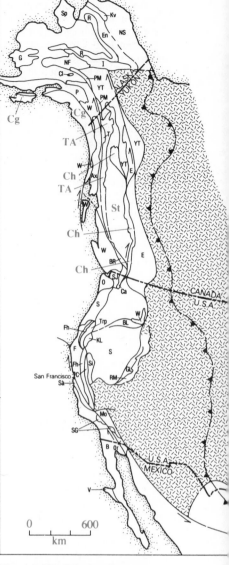

Figure 3.17 Displaced terrane of western North America; those discussed in the text are Ch, Cache Creek; St, Stikine; TA, Tracey Arm; Cg, Chugach. Barbed line indicates the eastern limit of Cordilleran Mesozoic–Cenozoic deformation in western North America and half-headed arrows give directions of strike–slip motions.

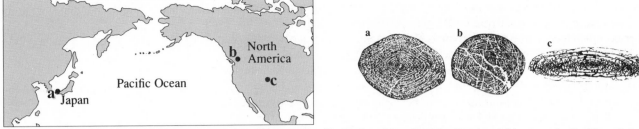

Figure 3.18   Fossil evidence for the transportation of western Pacific (Tethyan) fusulinid fossils (a) and (b) across the Pacific and their incorporation into North American terranes, where indigenous fusulinids are quite different (c). It is inferred that the fossils were incorporated prior to terrane migration, and that whole lithospheric blocks have therefore been transported across the Pacific.

during the collisions of India with Asia and Africa with Europe: the eastern end evolved into the site of the younger Jurassic–Recent Pacific Ocean. The implications for the origin of the Cache Creek terrane are clear.

What do you think they are? How did Cache Creek originate?

Cache Creek is believed to have formed part of the ocean floor of Tethys receiving late Palaeozoic carbonate sediments, to have migrated across the early Pacific, and is assumed to have been accreted onto the margin of North America. This simple explanation for the fusulinid evidence carries important implications, for the exotic fusulinid-bearing rocks are found as far as 500 km inland from the present Pacific coast of North America, implying that all the material to the west of them has also arisen as displaced terranes. As noted earlier, this is just part of the evidence on which the interpretation in Figure 3.17 is based.

Coney and Jones believe that the palaeogeography and plate movements since late Palaeozoic times were particularly appropriate for the accretion of terranes to North America. In a 1980 *Nature* article, with James Monger of the Canadian Geological Survey, they concluded:

> 'During late Palaeozoic and early Mesozoic time two-thirds of our planet's surface was paved with an enormous single ocean (Tethys). The other third was Pangea (an all-embracing supercontinent). Assuming that lengths and spacings of spreading centres were similar then to that now, a single large ocean would statistically favour more percentage area of old ocean crust lying around ready to be subducted than at any other time before or since the Phanerozoic. If offshore and/or intra-oceanic arcs correlate with subduction of cold or dense old oceanic crust, as has been suggested, large parts of the late Palaeozoic–early Mesozoic palaeo-Pacific Ocean could have been festooned with magmatic arcs. As Pangea began to break up and North America began to advance over that ocean, the arcs could have been swept northwards against large sectors of North America's margin to produce most of the Cordilleran mosaic which has been considered here. During this process, the Pacific was cleared of older arcs, oceanic plateaux and continental fragments, leading thus to the creation of the simple plate configuration that characterizes the present eastern Pacific.'

So the terranes of western North America result from 'sweeping clean' the continental fragments of the eastern Pacific. How reasonable is the eloquent theory posed in the last sentence; how wide was the eastern Pacific?

ITQ 3.7   We know from the oldest part of the western Pacific, adjacent to Japan, that the Pacific Ocean has existed for at least 150 Ma and that spreading rates must have averaged at least 4 cm a^{-1} during that time.

(a) What length of oceanic lithosphere must have been consumed beneath coastal California?

(b) Could this oceanic lithosphere have carried fragments of *continent* originally on the western side of the Pacific? If so, how?

(c) Does this leave you feeling convinced that the conclusions reached by Coney, Jones and Monger might be right? Why, in particular, do they expect young island arcs to be available for accretion along with older continental fragments?

70

Finally, if terrane accretion due to 'closure' of half an ocean — the eastern Pacific — is so obvious in the geological framework of North America, surely we must find even more complicated terrane accretion areas in ancient suture zones where two continental plates have closed over a former ocean basin. This is precisely what is now being discovered, providing a new and revolutionary explanation for previously unexplained geological discontinuities in intra-continental mountain belts. Not only are there strong vertical tectonic movements between adjacent blocks to consider, but lateral displacements too, and if western North America is to be taken as an example, we might expect large movements *parallel* to continental margins. Just as an example — which we shall not discuss in detail — look at Figure 3.19, which represents a recent interpretation of terranes across the 300 km wide zone of Lower Palaeozoic sutures of NE Canada between the Canadian shield to the northwest and the Atlantic province to the southeast. This is just one section through a much more extensive zone, which extends southwest along the Appalachian mountains of eastern North America in one direction, and through the British Isles out to Scandinavia in the other direction. Remember that this is a Lower Palaeozoic collision zone and that the North Atlantic dates from 50–60 Ma ago, so the Appalachian and Caledonian mountains formed a continuous chain for most of the last 400 Ma.

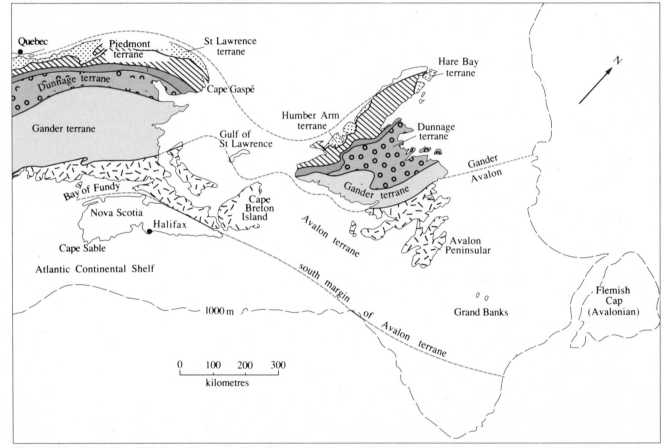

Figure 3.19   Map of the NE Canadian part of the Caledonian–Appalachian mountain belt formed in the Lower Palaeozoic by the suturing of two former continents, represented here by the Canadian Shield and the Atlantic continental shelf. Note the complexity of the elongate (parallel to the orogenic belt) displaced terranes that have been recognized. From east to west, these are the Avalon, Gander, Dunnage and Piedmont terranes, though several other smaller terrane blocks are also included. Note that the outer margin of the area considered here is the 1 000 m ocean depth contour at the edge of the continental shelf.

In the next Section, we shall revise some of the information introduced in previous Courses about the *Caledonian orogeny* of Britain, and then look again at the terrane concept in relation to the whole of this continental collision zone.

Summary

In Section 3.3, we have introduced the concept that discrete blocks of continental lithosphere, known as terranes, are often subject to large-scale horizontal displacements across the Earth's surface before they become accreted to a continental plate boundary. Once again, our concept of simple, uniform-geometry continental plates moving about the Earth's surface requires some revision. In particular:

1   The geometry of individual terrane blocks can be extremely diverse, depending on their origin and subsequent tectonic development. There are four particularly important factors:

(i) The localization of the extensional stress regimes that fragment continents and create new terrane blocks from old lithosphere.

(ii) In the case of island-arc systems, the geometry of any nearby continental plate margin, of the subduction zone itself, and the age of the oceanic lithosphere.

(iii) The nature of terrane motions across an oceanic plate, often involving extensive strike–slip movement guided by oceanic transforms.

(iv) The geometric relationship between the plate motion vectors at the accreting continental boundary (for example, transpression causes shearing, which is reflected in the elongate terrane geometry of the western North American accretion zone — Figure 3.17).

Clearly, because of their diverse origins, the recognition of terranes depends on geological differences as well as their differences in geometry.

2   The accretion process itself is related to convergence at ocean–continent boundaries, where any unsubductable continental terranes, riding on the oceanic plate, are swept onto the margins of the advancing continent(s). Terrane accretion is increasingly recognized as a feature of intra-continental collision zones where a whole ocean has disappeared (see, for example, Figure 3.19). The preservation of abrupt terrane boundaries in such areas therefore provides important evidence for *ancient* collision zones where continents have become sutured. Their geometric, geological and palaeomagnetic characteristics may be used to reconstruct scenarios for the plate tectonic evolution of the ancient oceans that have long since disappeared.

3.4   THE TECTONIC EVOLUTION OF THE BRITISH ISLES

In Britain, we are extremely fortunate as geologists to live in a relatively small area of continental lithosphere characterized by geological and tectonic processes of great diversity and complexity. For example, the Lewisian metamorphic basement of NW Scotland records thermal events as old as 2 900 Ma on the one hand, while, on the other, the adjacent Tertiary igneous province extending from St Kilda and Skye in the north, through NE Ireland, to Lundy in the Bristol Channel is only 50–60 Ma old. Much of the geology of central and northern Britain is strongly influenced by continental collision events of Caledonian age, culminating about 400 Ma ago, while a later 270 Ma, Variscan collisional event affected much of southern Britain. At various times in the past, much of Britain has been a continental landmass receiving a cover of subaerial sedimentary deposits; for example, in the late Precambrian of Scotland and, more recently, in the Devonian and Permo-Triassic. At other times, shallow shelf seas have covered much of the land, and this occurred, especially in southern Britain, during the Carboniferous, and again in various places since the Jurassic. Finally, deeper water deposits occur in the collision zones mentioned above. As you know, extensional tectonic processes, active at various times, were responsible for creating the North Sea Basin structure, while the Tertiary igneous province marks a line of extension and of lithospheric separation to the southeast of the final site of opening of the North Atlantic. The Midland Valley of Scotland is another extension zone, which we shall be considering in Block 2.

So there is abundant evidence of the past dynamic plate tectonic history of Britain, and, again, perhaps it is fortunate that for the past 50 Ma, we have been part of a stable region of continental lithosphere with no volcanoes or major earthquakes. All the features mentioned above were discussed in detail, using the 10 mile geological maps (10 miles to 1 inch) of the United Kingdom, in an earlier course. Here, we are concerned with revising the broad tectonic framework and then focusing on key features of Caledonian events in the UK.

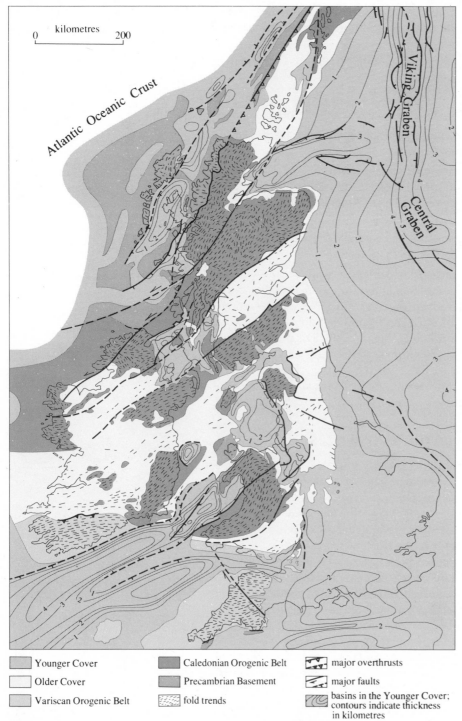

Figure 3.20 The main structural features and the distribution of the five principal lithotectonic units in the British Isles.

3.4.1 The tectonic framework

The major structural and lithotectonic units (i.e. rock units characterized by similarities of lithology and tectonic history) of Britain are illustrated in Figure 3.20, which you will need to study carefully. First, concentrate on the *Younger Cover*, which includes strata of generally post-Carboniferous age — mainly Mesozoic and Cenozoic sedimentary rocks but including the igneous complexes of western Scotland and Northern Ireland. In most cases, the sedimentary rocks are either horizontal or gently dipping, and they lie with a marked angular discordance on older units which have usually been more extensively folded. The development of the Younger Cover was strongly influenced by (i) erosional and depositional processes following uplift due to the Variscan collisional events, (ii) a global rise of sea-level that occurred during the Mesozoic, creating shelf-seas over many low-lying continental areas, and

(iii) tectonic events associated with the opening of the Atlantic Ocean. Notice that most onshore areas have a relatively thin veneer of Younger Cover (e.g. eastern England where there is *c*. 1 km of cover) but offshore areas can contain much greater thickness, up to 9 km.

> How do you account for these large differences, bearing in mind that, apart from Atlantic oceanic crust, the whole of the area in Figure 3.20 is underlain by continental lithosphere?

The offshore areas are sedimentary basins, which, in general, are elongate normal fault-bounded structures (except for the Hampshire Basin) that were probably produced by Permian and, more recently, Mesozoic extensional tectonics. Examples occur in the southwest approaches, the grabens of the northern North Sea and the Sea of the Hebrides (between the Hebridean Islands and mainland Scotland). As you know, these offshore sedimentary basins have been discovered during extensive exploration programmes for oil and gas.

In contrast, *Older Cover* is confined to surface outcrops mainly in onshore areas of Britain, though it also forms the floor of the western Irish Sea and extends from mainland Scotland through to the Shetlands. The Older Cover consists of a series of broadly conformable Devonian and Carboniferous strata, which rest with a marked angular discordance on rocks of the Caledonian Orogenic Belt, or are faulted against it. The most significant faults are those bounding the Midland Valley rift of Scotland — they are the northeast–southwest trending Highland Boundary Fault to the north and Southern Uplands Fault to the south. Some folds also occur bringing Older Cover rocks to the surface along anticlinal axes such as the north–south trending Pennine axis. Extensive outcrops of volcanic rocks occur within this Older Cover lithotectonic unit, particularly in the Midland Valley of Scotland.

The Variscan Orogenic Belt consists of intensely deformed, greenschist metamorphic facies strata of late Palaeozoic age exposed in SW England. To the north of the main belt, in south Wales and the Mendips, the intensity of folding decreases, but it is still much greater than in the cover rocks just described. This makes it rather difficult to define precisely the boundary between the Variscan Orogenic Belt and the Older Cover. Structural geologists take the northernmost limit of the belt, known as the **Variscan Front** (see Figure 3.21) as the line up to which deformed rocks have been carried by northerly-directed Variscan thrusting. In other words, it is a thrust front beyond which gentle folding due to Variscan events continues. It is clear from a combination of surface geological and geophysical observations, some of which will be described in Block 1B, that the Variscan Front occurs at or near the surface within southern Ireland (see Figure 3.20), clips the southernmost parts of Wales and then extends east, beneath this Younger Cover, across the London Basin and out into central France. The four lithotectonic zones shown in Figure 3.21 (whose names you need not remember!) are separate thrust terranes all occurring to the north of an east–west suture zone, detectable at the surface in the Massif Central of southern France. Beneath these terranes was a northwards-dipping subduction zone, and some workers believe that back-arc marginal basins developed in the northern (Rheno–Hercynian) terrane, including Cornwall. Further details of Variscan structures associated with collision in southern Europe are greatly complicated by subsequent Alpine orogenic events and need concern us no further in this Block.

> Returning to SW England, various igneous rocks occur in the Variscan province. Can you recall what these are and what might be their tectonic significance?

The main igneous rocks are large granite masses, which crop out down the spine of the Variscan province through Devon and Cornwall, and which are known from gravity data to be part of a much more extensive batholith with deep roots (see Block 1B). An important, but isolated occurrence of mafic–ultramafic material, carried on the back of a thrust, occurs in the Lizard area of southern Cornwall. Both the granites and the Lizard Complex — which is interpreted as a fragment of oceanic lithosphere, an *ophiolite complex,* now trapped in a collisional terrane — are characteristic of continental collision zones. However, there are no andesites in SW

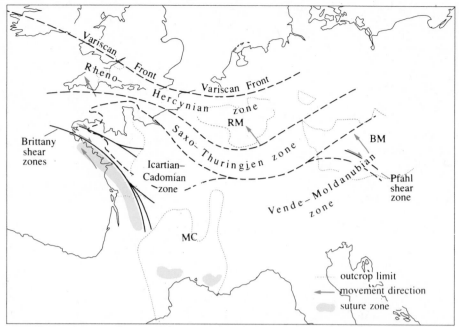

Figure 3.21 The Variscan fold-thrust belt of SW Britain and W Europe showing the location of the Variscan Front and thrust terranes north of an east–west suture zone inferred to occur at the surface in the French Massif Centrale (MC). RM, Rhenish Massif; BM, Bavarian Massif.

England, and it is envisaged, in some of the many tectonic models for this province, that the granite magmas were generated at a destructive margin well to the south of Britain and were then injected northwards to produce a *sheet* with an irregular upper surface. This is necessary because geological evidence shows that the granites were emplaced after the main deformation. Figure 3.22 gives a simplified impression of the kind of thrusting that may have produced the immense structural complexity of the Variscan Orogenic Belt in Britain; it incorporates the Lizard ophiolite as a separate thrust sheet and allows for the lateral injection followed by vertical uprise of granite magma under the prevailing late-Variscan stress regime.

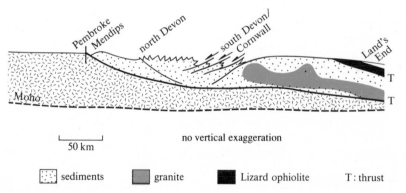

Figure 3.22 Possible cross-section through SW England showing low-angle thrusting of Variscan metasediments to the north over Older Cover. The Lizard ophiolite is carried by a separate thrust, and lateral injection of granite magma under the prevailing stress regime is thought to have been responsible for batholith emplacement. This cross-section shows the crust as it would have been in early Permian times, about 270 Ma ago.

A much more complete section through a zone of ancient continental collision is preserved within the *Caledonian Orogenic Belt* of Britain. The belt can be divided into two parts (see Figure 3.23): (i) to the north of the Highland Boundary Fault occur the *metamorphic Caledonides*, where greenschist and higher facies late Precambrian to Ordovician metasediments of the Moine and Dalradian show complex compressive thrusting and fold deformation; (ii) to the south, from the Southern Uplands Fault southward occur the *non-metamorphic Caledonides*, (which have undergone low-grade metamorphism) essentially a slate belt incorporating thick Lower Palaeozoic mudstones and sandstones which show evidence of gentler folding and deformation than in the north.

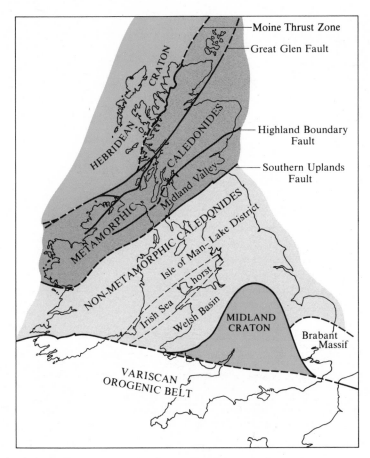

Figure 3.23 The principal zones of the British Caledonides.

In the Southern Uplands area, there is evidence for the development of an accretionary prism of sedimentary rocks caught in a collision zone. Various lines of evidence point to closure of the pre-400 Ma *Iapetus Ocean* along a line south of the Southern Uplands which passes through the Solway Firth and west to the Shannon Estuary of SW Ireland (further details in Section 3.4.2). Extensive zones of non-metamorphic Caledonian slates occur (i) in the Lake District, a dome-like structure which really is a major anticline with a northeast–southwest axis, (ii) in Wales and the Irish Sea horst, which again are best described as faulted major anticline–syncline structures with NE–SW axes, and (iii) in various parts of eastern and central Ireland (see Figure 3.20).

How do all these NE–SW fold axes relate to the prevailing tectonic stress regime during Caledonian events?

They are likely to reflect major compressive deformation associated with closure of the Iapetus Ocean along a NE–SW line as just described. By analogy with western North America today, of course, there may also have been strike–slip movements parallel to the plate boundary, and this is commonly invoked, particularly for movements on the Great Glen Fault.

What would we call this combination of compression and strike–slip deformation?

This is known as transpression — see Figure 3.5a — and we return to this in a Caledonian context shortly, in Section 3.4.2.

Finally, the Caledonides contain extensive tracts of granite outcrops, in the Scottish Highlands, the Southern Uplands and Northern England, but not in Wales. However, volcanic andesites and basaltic andesites occur in all these areas, and a strong case can be made for simple subduction-related magmatism around the margins of Iapetus. This case is examined critically and modified a little for the non-metamorphic Caledonian igneous rocks at the end of Block 3.

The final part of this preliminary examination of the tectonic framework of Britain is the *Precambrian Basement* lithotectonic unit (see Figure 3.20). The Basement consists of rocks that are either older than those of the Caledonian Orogenic Belt, or that were left unscathed by Caledonian events. In NW Scotland, major thrusts form the boundary between the Metamorphic Caledonides and the Basement where Moine metasedimentary rocks have been transported by Caledonian events to the northwest, across the ancient *Hebridean Craton* (Figure 3.23) which consists of Lewisian rocks. The *Moine Thrust Zone* is shown, together with some of the complex high-level structures of the metamorphic Caledonides, in Figure 3.24. In north Wales, the Welsh Borders and southern Ireland, the pre-Caledonian Basement lies unconformably beneath rocks of the orogenic belt and includes a wide variety of ancient metasedimentary and igneous rocks, generally of a Precambrian age (600–700 Ma), much younger than the (1 850–2 700 Ma) Lewisian of the Hebridean Craton. The extensive *Midland Craton* shown in Figure 3.23 is not well exposed, but from isolated outcrops in Leicestershire and the Welsh Borders, is also of this late Precambrian age and probably is continuous at depth with the Basement of North Wales and Southern Ireland. Clearly, two completely different pieces of continental lithosphere with contrasting tectonic histories were brought together by Caledonian events.

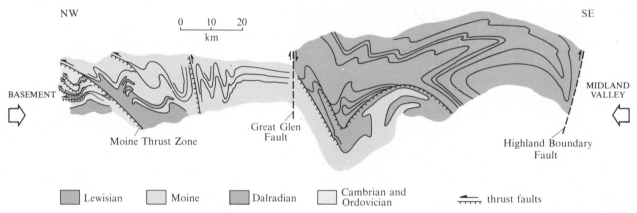

Figure 3.24 Sketch structural section showing the extent of crustal shortening across the metamorphic Caledonides in the Scottish Highlands. Note how the deformation patterns can be interpreted crudely in terms of squeezing between the Basement to the northwest, across which Caledonian rocks have been carried on the Moine Thrust, and the Midland Valley region to the southeast.

3.4.2 Caledonian plate tectonics

We will start in the northern, metamorphic Caledonides and will look for evidence of extensional and compressional processes in the Moine and Dalradian.

> **ITQ 3.8** Take a closer look at Figure 3.24, which gives an interpretation of the style of compressive deformation in the top few kilometres of the crust.
>
> (a) In what order were the original Moine and Dalradian sediments laid down?
>
> (b) What are the relative ages of the rocks above and below the Moine Thrust Zone?
>
> (c) Describe the style of faulting and folding in this section, noting, in particular, areas where the strata have become inverted.

We have evidence from radiometric dates on both mafic and granitic intrusions throughout the Moine and Dalradian that deformation and metamorphism occurred sporadically between 600 and 400 Ma ago. This represents a long history of multiple collisions and perhaps accretion of terranes to the northern margin of the Iapetus Ocean.

But what about extensional events; when did Iapetus open? The Moine meta-sediments represent a thick sequence of sandstones and shales laid down in a shallow marine environment rather than in a deep ocean. However, they are difficult rocks to date, though a metamorphism at 1 050 Ma ago has been recognized radiometrically. The Dalradian sequence contains much more useful clues, partly because the sedimentary sequence is more varied (Figure 3.25) and partly because the rocks are younger. The same shallow marine conditions persisted until around 650 Ma ago when a prominent tillite was deposited.

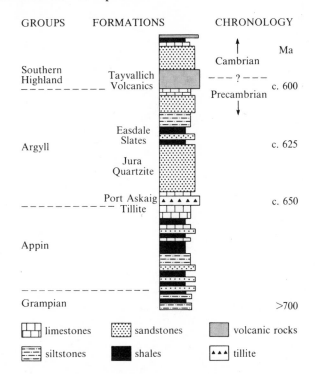

GROUPS	FORMATIONS	CHRONOLOGY

Southern Highland — Tayvallich Volcanics

Cambrian — Ma
--- ? ---
Precambrian — c. 600

Argyll — Easdale Slates — c. 625

Jura Quartzite

Port Askaig Tillite — c. 650

Appin

Grampian — >700

limestones   sandstones   volcanic rocks

siltstones   shales   tillite

Figure 3.25 The succession of rock units in the Dalradian. This is a composite section derived from studies in several areas; it encompasses at least 10 km of strata. Sections from different areas will be considered in Block 4.

Can you recall what is the significance of tillites?

These are sedimentary deposits of glacial origin, conditions in which matrix-supported conglomerates can be deposited. The significance of the Port Askaig tillite is that rocks of identical age in Scandinavia (on the opposite, southeast, side of the eventual Iapetus Ocean) exhibit similar ice-sheet lithologies, suggesting that an ocean had not yet formed. Moreover, above the tillite there is a progressively thickening sequence of metamorphosed sedimentary rocks, which indicates a period of rapid subsidence, with the former shallow subsiding shelf being broken into a series of blocks and basins: this is the Argyll group in Figure 3.25.

ITQ 3.9 What does this lithospheric fragmentation suggest about the probable stress regime, and is this supported by the component strata of the Southern Highland Dalradian group?

So one possible interpretation of the Tayvallich lavas, which are basaltic, is that they may be providing us with a record of the opening of Iapetus at 600 Ma ago. Thus, in a period of just 100 Ma, the Highland area was transformed from a passive continental margin with a shelf sea, to a continental rift zone and then to an orogenic belt. This is, perhaps, a surprisingly rapid series of developments, though, of course, an ocean the size of the present North Atlantic could open and close in just 100 Ma, and that at slow spreading rates of 2 cm a^{-1}, giving a maximum separation of 1 000 km per ridge flank. However, there is no clear evidence for a subduction zone and associated oceanic trench in the Highland area, so we must look south of the Highland Boundary Fault to understand more about the tectonic evolution of this northern Iapetus margin.

As there are only minor outcrops of Lower Palaeozoic rocks in the Midland Valley area, we examine next the Southern Uplands. The origin and deep structure of the Midland Valley will be considered again in Block 1B and Block 2. Figure 3.26a shows outcrops of Ordovician and Silurian rocks in the Southern Uplands, from which it is clear that, as in the Scottish Highlands, there is an overall younging to the southeast. Lithological sequences often show basalt and pyroclastic layers overlain by relatively thin cherts (fine-grained beds of amorphous silica), and/or black shales. These are followed by extremely thick sequences of greywacke turbidites.

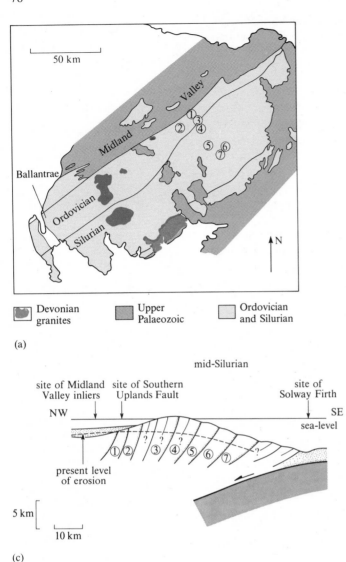

(a)

(c)

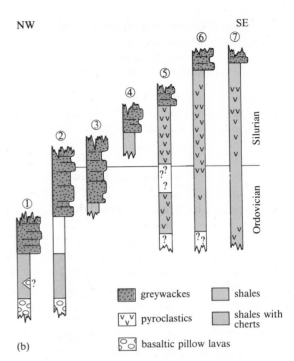

(b)

Figure 3.26 The Ordovician and Silurian rocks of the Southern Uplands (a) at outcrop, showing localities of successions within the fault blocks illustrated in (b), and a model for the development of the accretionary prism discussed in the text (c).

What kinds of depositional environments would be associated with these sediments.

Thin cherts and black shales indicate slow deposition of clastic material in relatively deep water, while the great thicknesses of coarse greywackes suggest rapid deposition associated with an unstable slope that triggered turbidity flows. Structurally, the Southern Uplands sequence is considerably shortened by isoclinal folding, and there are large thrust faults dipping to the northwest, which separate blocks within each of which the stratigraphic sequence differs slightly (Figure 3.26b). Notice, in particular, how the greywacke part of the sequence occurs slightly later further south. By analogy with modern accretionary plate margins, the cross-section in Figure 3.26c was proposed. It is suggested that a succession of slivers of sedimentary material, riding on the back of subducting oceanic lithosphere, were thrust beneath the continental margin to the northwest, forming an accretionary prism, and moving the site of the oceanic trench progressively to the southeast.

Does this account for the progressively *later* transition from volcanic to greywacke sedimentation from northwest to southeast (Figure 3.26b)?

The accretion process involved a time-span whereby sequence ① was accreted during the Ordovician, followed by sequence ②, and so on, to sequence ⑦ much later in the Silurian. So the greywacke turbidites must have formed relatively close to the northern shore of Iapetus and were then accreted one after the other in a process that continued throughout much of Ordovician and Silurian times. It appears that the accretion process ceased and that Iapetus closed, south of the Southern Uplands, towards the end of the Silurian period, around 400 Ma ago. (You should note that this is just one of the more popular models of many currently being debated concerning the origin of the Southern Uplands.)

This leaves us with a problem, because major compressional deformation in the Highlands had already been going on for 200 Ma! What sequence of extensional and compressional processes could account for this state of affairs? Some researchers have argued that the Iapetus Ocean was subject to a two-stage opening and closing cycle. The more popular view today is that transpressional accretion of terrane blocks onto the northern margin of Iapetus may have produced a series of deformational events. For example, John Dewey of Oxford, and Robert Shackleton of the Open University have recently argued that the Midland Valley basement seen in xenoliths brought up in Carboniferous volcanic vents has more in common with the younger Precambrian provinces of eastern Canada than the older northern Scottish basement. There are more slivers of this material caught up within the complex terranes of southwest Newfoundland (Figure 3.19). The Dewey/Shackleton view is that, from a common source in eastern Canada, the Midland Valley terrane was subject to lateral strike–slip displacement to the northeast along the northern Iapetus margin during the Silurian. This movement must have taken place along the Highland Boundary Fault, so any terranes that *were* adjacent to the Scottish Highlands would have been moved further northeast. Similar movements also occurred at different times along the Great Glen and Southern Uplands Faults (Figure 3.23). This leads to the conclusion that a series of terrane accretion and strike–slip motions may have dominated the northern margin of Iapetus, so it is perhaps not surprising that several stages of compressional deformation were involved. Although this is rather an unsatisfactory place to leave this incomplete story, remember that we shall be returning to the evolution of the Midland Valley and the Scottish Highlands in Blocks 2 and 4.

One final point about the Scottish non-metamorphic Caledonides; apart from the accretionary prism of basalt, pyroclastics and sedimentary clastic rocks in the Southern Uplands, there is a sequence of Ordovician, mafic and ultramafic rocks at Ballantrae (Figure 3.26a). At this locality, we are seeing part of the Ordovician floor of Iapetus that failed to become subducted; this is the *Ballantrae ophiolite*. A simple model for the late-stage evolution of Iapetus is shown in Figure 3.27: evidence for the Scottish part of this picture has now been given, but what about England and Wales, the rest of the non-metamorphic Caledonides (Figure 3.23)?

Figure 3.27 Model for the late-stage evolution of the Caledonian Orogenic Belt in Britain (a) prior to collision and (b) after collision, showing Carboniferous volcanics developing in the Midland Valley. Accurate cross-sections for earlier stages in this sequence are outside the scope of the arguments developed in this Block because the complexities of terrane accretion and strike–slip motion, particularly on the northern side of Iapetus need to be considered in more detail.

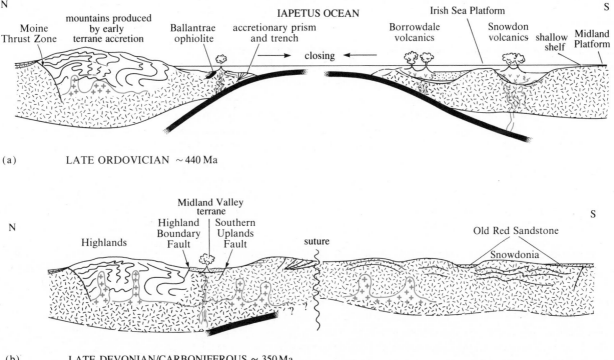

Moving south into the Lake District, there are many gross similarities in the range of rock types and their lack of high-grade metamorphism to the Southern Uplands sequences. The most striking differences are the occurrence in the Lake District of a thick series of andesitic volcanic rocks — the *Borrowdale Volcanic Group* — and the absence of thrust faulting and tight isoclinal folding.

> What does this suggest about the Lower Palaeozoic evolution of the Lake District — in terms of accretionary prisms and subduction?

Whereas the lack of thrusts suggests that accretionary prisms did not develop in the Lake District, the andesitic volcanics indicate that the area was situated above a subduction zone. Moreover, given that we have a northward dipping subduction zone in the Southern Uplands, with an ocean situated to the south, it is logical to assume that the Lake District volcanics result from subduction on the southern margin of Iapetus, as shown in Figure 3.27a. However, the Borrowdale Volcanics are of mid-Ordovician age, and, in contrast to the Southern Uplands, there is no evidence that subduction continued into the Silurian. Nevertheless, the last broad folds and rock cleavages developed in the Lake District are end-Silurian in age, suggesting, as in the Southern Uplands, that intra-continental collision may have occurred at this time.

While no pre-Ordovician rocks occur in the Lake District and, indeed, the whole of the Lake District–Southern Uplands area may have no older, pre-Ordovician continental basement, the area to the south, in Wales and the Midlands, has a late Precambrian metamorphic basement (cf. Figure 3.20). A wide variety of these older rocks is exposed in Anglesey and as intermittent outcrops in Shropshire and Leicestershire. Figure 3.28 illustrates the palaeogeography and rock successions encountered across this area: two upstanding areas, the Midland Platform and the Irish Sea Platform are identified with the Welsh Basin between.

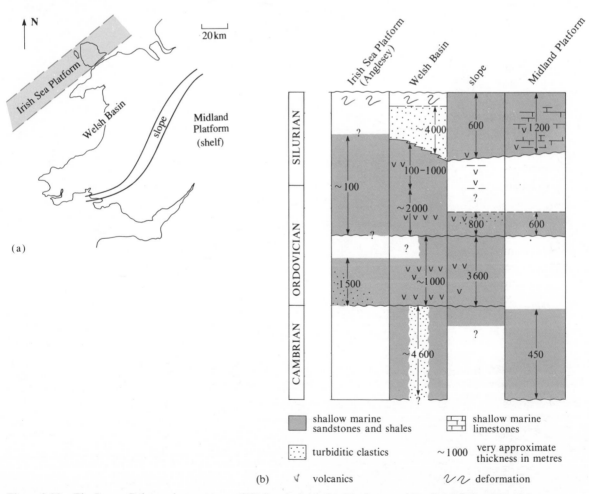

Figure 3.28 The Lower Palaeozoic sequences of Wales, the Irish Sea Platform and English Midland Platform; (a) palaeogeography, (b) typical successions.

ITQ 3.10   What are the differences between the Lower Palaeozoic sedimentation histories in the Welsh Basin, over the Irish Sea Platform and the Midland Platform? Consider this question in terms of (a) the presence of discontinuities in the rock record, (b) contrasts in thickness, and (c) the nature of the sediments.

What does this imply about tectonic processes during the Lower Palaeozoic in England and Wales?

The Irish Sea Platform remained high as surrounding areas subsided; it was an island that only became submerged intermittently during the Ordovician and Silurian. However, the Welsh Basin seems to have subsided continuously throughout the Lower Palaeozoic, accumulating 10 km of sediments and volcanics. The latter are of acid and intermediate composition; they span a time interval from Lower Ordovician to mid-Silurian, much longer than the volcanic episode in the Lake District. The Midland Platform was either emergent or only very slowly subsiding to judge from the thin sequences in Figure 3.28b in which there are also frequent breaks in the succession. It is therefore clear that Lower Palaeozoic conditions in Wales and the Midlands were those of a fault-controlled basin or basins separated from the Iapetus Ocean by a horst-like area — the Irish Sea Platform. To the northwest of the horst, in the Isle of Man and the Lake District, thick sedimentary sequences were deposited that may have formed on a continental slope and shelf flanking the open ocean, or in a basin situated behind an island arc.

In simple terms, it is convenient to think of two Ordovician volcanic arcs, one in the Lake District and one in Wales as shown in Figure 3.27a. Some researchers believe that there were two parallel subduction zones. Others regard the Welsh volcanic rocks as having been erupted in a tectonic environment transitional between an island arc and a marginal basin. Although back-arc spreading apparently did not occur in the Welsh Basin during the Lower Palaeozoic, the occurrence of such thick sedimentary sequences does suggest a process of lithospheric thinning and subsidence over a zone of sublithospheric melting, associated with subduction, beneath Wales. We shall be looking again at the tectonic history of the southern margin of Iapetus in Block 3. Both north and south of the region where the northern and southern plates come together — the Iapetus suture — are abundant granite batholiths, some of which are related directly to the subduction processes, as in the modern Andes, while some postdated subduction and have more complex origins — these are also considered in the context of modern ocean–continent and continent–continent convergent regimes in Blocks 3 and 4.

Finally, in this brief summary of Caledonian tectonics in Britain, what of the Iapetus suture itself? We have seen that there is evidence for northwards subduction beneath the Southern Uplands and southwards subduction beneath the Lake District and Wales. Thus it is reasonable to assume that the suture along which the two formerly separated continental masses were joined must occur somewhere in the Solway Firth area. This conclusion is reinforced by palaeontological and palaeomagnetic studies, and also by the results of deep seismic reflection profiling, as you will see in Block 1B. Similar structural, sedimentological and metamorphic zones to those of Scotland, England and Wales, are recognized in Ireland and, given the NE–SW 'structural grain' of the Caledonides, it is thought that the Iapetus suture crosses central Ireland to reach the west coast at the Shannon Estuary (the most prominent river estuary in W Ireland).

Thus the label 'non-metamorphic Caledonides' in Figure 3.23 roughly follows the Solway–Shannon line, our best estimate of the surface expression of the Iapetus suture. This is the line recognized in Figure 3.29, a reconstruction of Caledonian–Appalachian terrane palaeogeography in the Silurian, 30 Ma before closure. Note that, during the Silurian, only a northwards-dipping subduction zone is envisaged in Britain. Southern Britain and continental Europe formed part of the late Precambrian (as seen in Anglesey and the Midlands) **Cadomian terrane**, sometimes known as *Eastern Avalonia*. SE Newfoundland and the eastern Appalachians were part of a similar terrane, usually known as *Avalonia* (cf. Figure 3.29). At the end of Silurian times, these terranes docked with Laurentia, the ancient Precambrian craton

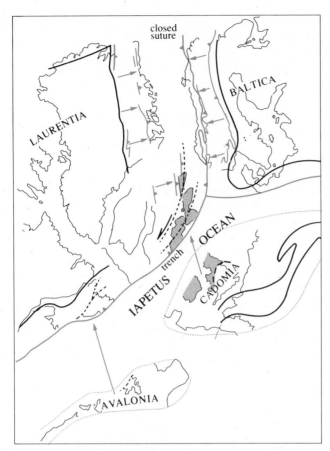

Figure 3.29   Reconstruction of the Caledonian–Appalachian terranes and Iapetus Ocean in mid-Silurian times. Collision has already taken place between Baltica and Laurentia, to the north, but within-plate deformation is continuing as indicated by the short red arrows. Cadomia has yet to collide with N Britain–S Baltica and Avalonia with the Appalachians. A 2 cm a^{-1} convergence rate has been assumed.

of North America and Greenland, including NW Scotland, to which the Midland Valley and Southern Uplands terranes had accreted. The northern boundary of Iapetus was subject to considerable strike–slip motions in an overall compressional regime: transpressional tectonics. Figure 3.29 also illustrates the relatively recent (mid-1980s) idea that a third major plate was involved, known as *Baltica*, which closed on Laurentia at an earlier stage than Cadomia, probably in late Ordovician–early Silurian times. Thus a prominent strike–slip boundary must have existed between Cadomia and Baltica, with a triple junction somewhere in the present-day North Sea area. To the east, the Iapetus Ocean gave way to a marine area separating Baltica and Cadomia which closed across central Europe — known as *Tornquist's Sea*. The significance of this ocean and of the three plate model for Caledonian tectonics will become clear in Block 1B.

Having now looked in some detail at the tectonic history of the British Caledonides as deduced from surface observations, the next step in this Course is to introduce some of the geophysical techniques used to gain a three-dimensional model of the lithosphere and its structure. This is the subject of Block 1B, in which we shall be using Britain as an example of how geophysical work can enhance the deductions made in this Section.

Summary

Section 3.4 has been entirely concerned with the tectonic framework of Britain as a prelude to our understanding of lithospheric evolution in this complex region as the Course proceeds. It includes many aspects that are revision from earlier courses, but incorporates some of the new concepts in plate tectonics introduced in Sections 3.1–3.3. The following points are of particular significance:

1   The tectonic history of Britain records significant convergent regimes in the Caledonian and Variscan Orogenic Belts (Figure 3.20). Between these periods, an Older Cover was developed, including mainly Devonian and Carboniferous strata. Post-Variscan strata are termed the Younger Cover; this conceals much of the tectonized basement in southern Britain, including the northern thrust limit of the Variscan Orogenic Belt, known as the Variscan Front (Figure 3.21).

2   The present shape of Britain has been moulded by extensional tectonic processes since the late Palaeozoic, creating the North Sea Basin and the 50–60 Ma old Tertiary igneous province, which also marks the line of continental rifting that led to the development of the North Atlantic.

3   Northern and central Britain record an almost complete section through the Caledonian Orogenic Belt which formed between 600 and 400 Ma ago, culminating in the closure of Iapetus along the Solway–Shannon line. The closure was preceded by the docking of various terrane blocks, notably the Midland Valley block, with its late Precambrian Basement, and the Southern Uplands accretionary prism (Figure 3.26), with notable strike–slip and associated compressional thrusting.

4   Away from the central region, early Caledonian processes in northern Scotland involved extensional tectonics and basaltic magmatism *c.* 600 Ma ago, possibly associated with the opening of Iapetus, followed by compressional tectonics over the next 200 Ma, producing the intense Moine–Dalradian deformation shown in Figure 3.24 and eventually the Moine Thrust.

5   To the south, in England and Wales, subduction-related magmatism was prominent during Ordovician times and an extensional subsiding basin formed in Wales between two positive blocks: the Irish Sea and Midland Platforms (Figure 3.28).

6   Differences in the age and nature of pre-Caledonian basement in southern Britain and Europe (Cadomia), the Appalachians (Avalonia), the Baltic region (Baltica) and the North American continent and NW Scotland (Laurentia) have led to the recognition of several major terrane blocks that existed in mid-Silurian times (Figure 3.29). These become united to form a large continental mass by 400 Ma ago, a mass that persisted until the modern Atlantic developed.

SAQS FOR SECTION 3

SAQ 3.1   With reference to Figure 3.3:

(a) What type(s) of plate boundaries surround the Antarctic Plate, and what does this imply for the probable changes in its size?

(b) Describe the stress regime operating due to plate motions in and around New Zealand (40° S, 170° E).

(c) Given your knowledge of plate motions in an absolute frame of reference, what will happen in the future to the length of the east–west convergent boundary joining the Atlantic Ridge to the Mediterranean Sea? Is this a simple convergent boundary? What processes are operating in this part of the Atlantic?

SAQ 3.2   State, with reasons, whether each of the following statements is true or false:

(a) Back-arc spreading is prevalent in marginal basins on the landward side of island arcs, particularly those beneath which oceanic lithosphere is being subducted rapidly.

(b) Arc–trench systems associated with back-arc spreading in marginal basins must migrate with time into the adjacent major ocean basin as the marginal basin grows.

(c) The stress regime that has caused extension in the Basin and Range Province of western North America has changed in sympathy with the tectonic evolution of the adjacent ocean–continent convergence zone of the Pacific margins.

(d) The Wernicke simple shear model of extensional tectonics involves deep faulting through normally ductile lithosphere along listric detachments, leading to an asymmetric distribution of normal fault blocks in the upper crust.

(e) The elongate nature of most displaced terranes recognized in convergent tectonic zones is a result of the enormous compressional stresses that deform lithospheric blocks during their migration.

SAQ 3.3   (a) Summarize the principal lines of evidence for the existence of shallow asthenosphere and for extensional tectonics in the Basin and Range Province.

(b) What is the likely consequence of the changing tectonic regime in western North America (cf. SAQ 3.2c) for the future evolution of the Basin and Range Province.

SAQ 3.4   (a) Explain what is meant by the Variscan Front as depicted in Figure 3.21, and account for the differences in metamorphism observed in SW England to either side of this boundary.

(b) Using the same criteria, where would you place the northern Caledonian Front in Figure 3.23 and the eastern Cordilleran Front of the western North America in Figure 3.17?

(c) What is the relationship between these fronts and the furthermost limit of displaced terranes in orogenic belts?

SAQ 3.5   Suppose you were asked to write an essay on the location of the Iapetus suture in Britain. Which *four* of the following topics would you think most relevant to the discussion and why?

(i)   The Moine Thrust Zone

(ii)   Volcanism in the Lake District and Wales

(iii)   Transpression across the Midland Valley

(iv)   Age and location of greywackes

(v)   Late Silurian–Devonian granites

(vi)   Subsidence of the Welsh Basin

(vii) Age and location of the Ballantrae ophiolite

(viii) Thrust directions in the Southern Uplands

(ix)   Age and distribution of Dalradian metamorphism

(x)   Laurentian, Cadomian and Avalonian basement rocks

(xi)   Fold structures in the Lake District

(xii)   Age and distribution of sedimentary rocks in the non-metamorphic Caledonides.

ITQ ANSWERS AND COMMENTS

ITQ 2.1 From equation 2.2, $K = \Delta d/t^{0.5}$, so using the linear part of the graph $K = 4500/12.8 \approx 350$ m Ma$^{-0.5}$.

The physical meaning of K is therefore that ocean depth increases by about 350 m for every unit increase in the square root of age, i.e. from 1 to 4 Ma, 4 to 9 Ma, 9 to 16 Ma, ..., 36 to 49 Ma, etc. Thus, as the age of ocean crust increases, the depth increases at a diminishing rate.

ITQ 2.2 (a) For the oceans to be more shallow than predicted by the $t^{0.5}$ model implies that the density beyond 60 Ma away from the ridge is less than predicted — lower density lithosphere occupies more volume. One possibility is that its chemical composition is different.

(b) Assuming uniform composition for the oceanic lithosphere, the internal temperatures of the lithosphere must be relatively constant, with horizontal isotherms, beyond 60 Ma from the ridge.

ITQ 2.3 (a) The adiabat crosses the solidus at *c.* 1 300 °C and 50 km depth; above this level, we must have partial melt. (Notice that any volatiles present may cause partial melting at even greater depths because the wet solidus is at a lower temperature than the dry solidus for any given depth or pressure.)

(b) In general terms, mantle partial melts are basalts. You will encounter more details of melting processes, products and conditions in Block 2.

(c) The extensional stress regime causes material to rise; this rising material carries heat upwards so that the isotherms are also bent upwards towards the ridge (cf. Figure 2.5). Only slight cooling along the adiabat occurs during ascent. The degree of melting must increase if the adiabat is followed all the way to the surface (i.e. further into the zone of partial melting to the right of the solidus in Figure 2.9).

ITQ 2.4 (a) The line passes through the origin of the graph, so there is no intercept. The gradient is 0.6, derived from the fact that q^* reaches 60 mW m^{-2} when $\bar{q}$ reaches 100 mW m^{-2}. So the equation must be $q^* = 0.6\,\bar{q}$: in words, the reduced heat flow is 0.6 of the mean heat flow.

(b) It follows that about 40% of mean continental heat flow arises from within the upper crustal radioactive layer, leaving 60% coming from greater depths.

ITQ 2.5 (a) See Table A1 for completed version of Table 2.2. (Don't worry if you couldn't read off the temperatures to this accuracy from Figure 2.12).

Table A1 (Completed version of Table 2.2)

Mean heat flow mW m^{-2}	Lithosphere thickness/km	Lithosphere basal temperature/°C
100	70	1 320
75	100	1 340
60	110	1 350
40	210	1 400
30	320	1 470

(b) To judge from Table A1, a mean heat flow of 57 mW m^{-2} would be associated with a lithosphere thickness rather greater than 110 km, probably of about 125 km. The youngest crustal provinces (< 250 Ma old) would have a lithosphere thickness of 100 km, and the oldest provinces (> 1 700 Ma old) about 180 km. There is a general thickening of continental lithosphere with increasing age.

ITQ 2.6 (a) The Moho is easily identified as the depth of rapid velocity increase at 30–40 km depth on both profiles. The top of the transition zone is coincident on both profiles where there is a sharp velocity increase of about 5% at just over 400 km depth.

(b) Between 30 km and 400 km depth, the two profiles differ, with the TNA S-wave velocity being less than that in SNA by a maximum of 10% at *c.* 125 km depth. The low velocity zone in the tectonic region is focused at this depth. In contrast, the shield has a thick high velocity 'lid', a relatively sharp low velocity area around 200 km depth and a shallower velocity gradient than TNA from 200 to 400 km depth. The two profiles approach each other across this region but do not coincide at depths shallower than 400 km. The minimum upper mantle S-wave velocity is recorded in tectonic areas at 125 km.

ITQ 2.7 (a) The following are based on a strain rate of 10^{-16} s^{-1}.

wet quartz	250 °C
dry quartz	280 °C
anorthite (Ca-feldspar)	425 °C
diopside (Ca-Mg pyroxene)	500 °C
olivine	750 °C

(b) The 425 °C temperature required for anorthite to become ductile occurs at nearly 25 km depth along this geotherm, so feldspar will not be ductile in the upper part of the crust. However, if quartz started to deform ductilely then the rocks would be strained. This requires temperatures of 250–300 °C which are reached at about 13–15 km depth in the crustal section specified. This is rather deep for quartz-rich upper crust but, nevertheless, *some ductile deformation could perhaps occur.*

The upper mantle is dominantly olivine, so we are looking for 750 °C which occurs at *c.* 50 km depth on the 60 mW m^{-2} geotherm. *So most of the continental mantle lithosphere will be ductile if subject to an extensional stress of 50 MPa at 60 mW m^{-2}.*

ITQ 2.8 (a) Quartz (upper crust) and anorthite (lower crust) reach threshold strain rates at 250–280 °C and 425 °C respectively (ITQ 2.7 and Figure 2.22). The high heat flow geotherms in Figure 2.12 have high geothermal gradients and are much less curved within the crust so reaching the temperatures at which quartz and anorthite will strain, respectively, at shallower and *much* shallower depths. For example, along the 100 mW m^{-2} geotherm, both anorthite and quartz reach ductile strain rates in the upper crust; quartz at about 6 km depth and anorthite at about 12 km. So at 100 mW m^{-2} there would be no elastic lower crust under an extensional stress of 50 MPa. However, there will always be a thin, near surface zone where quartz is cool enough to remain elastic until overtaken by the downwards migrating brittle zone.

(b) This occurs because (from Figure 2.23b) even the upper crustal elastic layer is breaking down after 1 Ma at 10 MPa stress if the heat flow is 90 mW m^{-2}. So, as the whole stress on the lithosphere is accumulated here, just above the depth of the threshold temperature for quartz to become ductile, the crust cannot sustain these stresses and breaks by brittle fracture.

ITQ 2.9 The earlier discussion of Figure 2.22 indicated that, under extension, olivine and feldspar reach geologically meaningful strain rates at much higher temperatures (*c.* 750 and 425 °C) than quartz (250–280 °C) which is important in the uppermost continental lithosphere. Indeed, the whole upper 35 km of the lithosphere will deform at lower temperatures in the continents than the oceans. So the oceanic lithosphere will be less susceptible to internal deformation under otherwise equal conditions: it is *much stronger* than continental lithosphere.

ITQ 2.10 (a) At high strain rates, thermal equilibrium will not be maintained and the transient geotherm (Figure 2.32b) applies. The whole lithosphere is cooler and thicker at this stage, and this must make it more resistant to deformation; thus the process of crustal shortening at high strain rates leads to strain hardening — it is clearly self-limiting.

(b) At low strain rates, we can achieve more deformation, in theory at least, because the *crust* is now thicker with higher temperatures near the base, and there will be only high-temperature mantle. As argued in relation to Figure 2.31, this is a strain-softening process, which, again in theory, could continue indefinitely *provided* strain rates remain low.

ITQ 3.1

	(i) Speed of plate motion	(ii) Direction of plate motion
(a) American Plate fixed	$4 \, cm \, a^{-1}$	east
(b) Australian Plate fixed	$4 \, cm \, a^{-1}$	west

(c) If Africa is fixed, both the American and Australian plates must be moving, respectively, west and east, both at $4 \, cm \, a^{-1}$ in this example. So in an absolute frame of reference, the Mid-Atlantic Ridge itself must be moving west at $2 \, cm \, a^{-1}$ and the Carlsberg Ridge east at $2 \, cm \, a^{-1}$.

ITQ 3.2 (a) The point of intersection between three plates, such as occurs at 105°W on the equator is known as a *triple junction*.

(b) The Pacific–Cocos and Pacific–Nazca plate boundaries clearly behave as divergent spreading ridges which dominate plate motion vectors further east. From the analysis in Figure 3.5c, we can deduce that the magnitude of the easterly spreading component due to these spreading ridges is about the same in both the Cocos and Nazca Plates. This is the origin of the easterly-directed components of strike–slip motion adjacent to the Cocos–Nazca boundary.

(c) The Cocos–Nazca boundary is a leaky transform, and thus has the characteristics of both a spreading ridge and a transform fault. This implies that at the three-plate intersection we have an RRR triple junction; characteristically, these are completely stable (see text following ITQ 3.2 if this is not clear to you). Since in this case, the transform fault appears to be present only because of different overall spreading vectors in the two adjacent plates and seems unlikely to disrupt the triple junction, it is probable that this particular plate configuration is stable (i.e. it will not change in character as spreading continues).

ITQ 3.3 (a) The β factor would locally exceed 1.5, and the heat flow would be high, greater than c. 90 mW m^{-2} (Section 2.2.3 and Figure 2.30). Remember that this implies that strain softening must have occurred at fast strain rates, so that melts from partially molten asthenosphere could reach the surface.

(b) An extension of 50% in 1 Ma (3.15×10^{13} s) requires a strain rate of 1.6×10^{-14} s^{-1} whereas 100% extension requires 3.2×10^{-14} s^{-1}. As Figure 2.30 confirms, such rapid strain rates are easily capable of propagating a continental lithosphere extension zone to $\beta > 1.5$ (i.e. consistent with part a).

ITQ 3.4 (a) The western limit of the BRP extension zone is formed by the Sierra Nevada mountains and the large Cretaceous subduction-related granite batholith to the east of them, both forming part of the late Mesozoic compressional mountain belt.

(b) Tertiary lavas provide valuable markers of rotational and vertical displacements due to extension, largely because they were originally erupted to form widespread horizontal layers at almost uniform topographic elevation (e.g. the Columbia River basalts).

(c) 1 400 Ma old gneisses have been brought to the surface in the core complex by a process called isostatic uplift in the programme and described in the preceding text as tectonic uplift: both descriptions are satisfactory. According to the evidence from high pressure metamorphic minerals, these rocks may once have been buried at 20 km depth in the crust.

(d) The programme regards the BRP as an active rift, stating near the end that the heat source of the East Pacific Rise (the Pacific–Farallon spreading ridge of Figure 3.7) was 'shoved' beneath the BRP causing extension within the continental plate.

ITQ 3.5 (a) In the Central Graben area studied by McKenzie's group, a two-stage extension history, both periods involving pure shear, was proposed with 30 km extension in the Permo-Triassic and 70 km extension in Jurassic times. The main extensional axes of the two basins are not superimposed, that for the youngest being offset to the west.

(b) On the McKenzie model, the highest heat flow occurs over the centre of the main basin, whereas, according to Wernicke's model, it occurs over the zone of maximum mantle lithosphere thinning (e.g. towards the right of Figure 3.14).

(c) According to the programme, the inferred presence of deep low-angle listric detachments, for example, beneath the Viking Graben, and of small-scale half graben structures which reflect an inherent asymmetry combine to make the Wernicke model more suitable for the interpretation of these northern North Sea structures. (Note that since the programme was made, some doubts have been voiced over the interpretation of the Viking Graben using the Wernicke model; nevertheless, the model still has many proponents.)

ITQ 3.6 (a) 75 Ma ago the Carlsberg and Southeast Indian Ridges were connected around the south and west coast of India by some large transform offsets, but the largest transforms were developed adjacent to the African and east Indian coastlines. Major northeast movement on the northeast side of the combined ridges produced new ocean lithosphere and thus forced India to the northeast between the transform 'tramlines'. By 35 Ma ago, the Southeast Indian Ridge had extended to separate Antarctica from Australia; the whole ridge system had migrated northeast relative to Africa (note the extended transform-like connection between the Southeast and Southwest Indian Ridges in Figure 3.16b); and more ocean had formed to the northeast of the Carlsberg–Southeast Indian Ridge system. Both the northeast migration and northeast spreading from this ridge system moved India further in this direction.

(b) Major subduction-suction (F_{SU}) stress was probably involved, whereby the oceanic lithosphere of Tethys, to the northeast of India, was under extensional stress due to subduction beneath Asia, and this may have been combined with compressional stress acting in the same direction and induced by the ocean ridge system (F_{RP}).

ITQ 3.7 (a) $4 \, cm \, a^{-1}$ for 150 Ma gives a total length of 6 000 km — implying a huge area of ocean, almost twice the width of the present Atlantic. Note that with the ocean ridge now having reached California, the whole of this length has been subducted — except for the continental fragments!

(b) By analogy with the splitting away of India from the southern continents (Figure 3.16), any continental fragments separated during initial extension of the continental lithosphere must lie on the opposite side of the new ocean ridge from the main continental mass (in this case the Eurasian and Australasian block). Any such separated fragments would remain on the eastern side of the Pacific ridge and become swept up by the Americas, moving west. (As you may realize, the situation is even more complicated because the modern Pacific grew from the eastern end of Tethys: North America and Asia have never been joined along their present Pacific coastlines).

(c) Given the large area of ocean available for subduction (a), and the possibility that continental fragments could be carried on the eastern Pacific plate, the Coney, Jones and Monger model seems satisfactory. They argue that old ocean lithosphere must have been present in the eastern Pacific presumably before North America overrode this part of the ocean, in which case the lithosphere may have become sufficiently dense to fail, subduct and form island arcs, which would also become accreted.

ITQ 3.8 (a) The Moine rocks are older than the Dalradian, as seen from their juxtaposition to the southeast of the Great Glen Fault — note that the strata here are not inverted.

(b) The Moine rocks are younger than the Lewisian Basement, but the particular section shown in Figure 3.24 brings Moine rocks on the back of the thrust over Cambrian and Ordovician. It is probable that in this area the relative ages are in reverse chronological order due to the effects of thrusting.

(c) According to this section, we have low-angle thrust faults to the northwest and reverse (compressional) faulting elsewhere (e.g. along the Highland Boundary Fault). Folding varies from isoclinal in the Moines to recumbent and nappe-like in the Dalradian with a large overturned section in the southeast, adjacent to the Highland Boundary Fault.

ITQ 3.9   The break-up into blocks and basins is a classic sign of extensional tectonics (cf. Section 3.2), and the appearance of volcanic rocks around 600 Ma ago suggests that strain rates were high, leading to possible sea-floor creation and spreading.

ITQ 3.10   (a) The Lower Palaeozoic of the Welsh Basin is virtually complete, whereas there are significant gaps over the Irish Sea Platform (Cambrian and Upper Silurian missing) and the Midlands Platform (most of the Ordovician and the Lower Silurian missing).

(b) The Welsh Basin accumulated over 10 000 m of sediment and volcanics during the Early Palaeozoic, in contrast to the thinner, incomplete successions elsewhere.

(c) Turbidites are confined to the Welsh Basin, and Ordovician volcanics also only occur in this area and the adjoining slope, with minor amounts in the Silurian of the Midland Platform, and over the Irish Sea Platform.

SAQ ANSWERS AND COMMENTS

SAQ 2.1   This is because heat flow (q) *decreases* with the square root of time (t) whereas oceanic depth (d) *increases* with the square root of time.

(ii) They are proportionality constants: C is the thermal–time constant describing the decay of heat flow with time, and K is the ocean depth–time constant.

(iii) The units of C are expressed in terms of $qt^{0.5}$, i.e. $W\,m^{-2}\,Ma^{0.5}$. The units of K are expressed in terms of $dt^{-0.5}$, i.e. $m\,Ma^{-0.5}$. (In case you find the units of C confusing, note that if heat flow is $0.1\,W\,m^{-2}$ ($100\,mW\,m^{-2}$) after 16 Ma, the value of C is $0.1 \times 4 = 0.4\,W\,m^{-2}\,Ma^{0.5}$. Thus, heat flow will be $0.08\,W\,m^{-2}$ after 25 Ma, $0.067\,W\,m^{-2}$ after 36 Ma, etc. The simpler case of K is explained in the answer to ITQ 2.1.)

(iv) If, instead of $350\,m\,Ma^{-0.5}$, the value of K were $700\,m\,Ma^{-0.5}$, this would mean that twice the contraction of the oceanic lithosphere was taking place in each time interval (1–4, 4–9, 9–16 Ma, etc.). This would imply, all other things being equal, that a thicker column of lithosphere (on the plate model) was available for contraction. So the simple answer is: this value of K implies about twice the lithosphere thickness.

(b) These relationships hold good for lithosphere less than about 60 Ma old, after which the heat flow is higher and the ocean floor depth shallower (Figure 2.3) than they predict. To account for these observations, it is believed that small-scale convection in the asthenosphere maintains a uniform thermal structure in older lithosphere (see also ITQ 2.2).

SAQ 2.2   On the plate model, there is a uniform thickness and basal temperature (125 km at 1 350 °C), so the decline in heat flow must result from the within-plate isotherms falling gradually until a uniform thermal gradient is established after 60 Ma (Figure 2.5). On the boundary layer model, the plate thickens with time, and the decline in surface heat flow results from the same heat flow being maintained at the base of the thickening plate. (Apart from adiabatic effects, this is the equivalent to maintaining the same basal temperaure — cf. Figure 2.6a). Both models reflect quite accurately the thermal structure of the lithosphere, but the lower parts of the plate model must be inelastic beneath ridge zones, so the boundary layer model best describes the lithosphere if it is defined as the rigid mechanical boundary layer plus the upper part of the thermal boundary layer.

SAQ 2.3   (a) Rising plumes would be associated with anomalously low density upper mantle, so creating large-scale negative gravity anomalies over ridge zones. Seasat radar altimeter data do not record a clear association between the corresponding topographic highs on the ocean surface and spreading ridges.

(b) The ocean ridges are zones of net extensional stress, mainly derived from the large forces associated with subduction of dense oceanic lithosphere into the mantle (F_{SP} in Figure 2.8), perhaps in combination with F_{RP}, sliding away from elevated ridge zones.

The combination of (a) and (b) suggests that many oceanic ridges may be passive zones of lithospheric extension and rifting, where adiabatically ascending asthenospheric material undergoes partial melting, so supplying the magmas that form oceanic crust (cf. Figure 2.10).

SAQ 2.4   (a) The depth of the boundary is determined by extrapolating downwards the conductive (upper) part of the geotherm until it intersects the upwards projected convective part of the geotherm. (The latter represents the temperature path followed by adiabatic asthenospheric mantle rising without heat loss — its temperature falls because of decompression. This definition gives a lithosphere base falling within the thermal boundary layer.)

(b) The thickness of the continental lithosphere at 60 Ma age is less because of higher heat production within the upper continental crust, which gives a curved, convex-upwards geotherm (Figure 2.12) and a higher heat flow than in the oceans at 60 Ma age. Analytically, we can show from the heat flow–heat production correlation for continental provinces (Figure 2.11a) that reduced heat flow from beneath the radiothermal layer amounts to c. 60% of mean heat flow (see Figure 2.11b and ITQ 2.4). This points to the importance of heat production in the crust, which may account for the remaining 40% of observed heat flow. (Award yourself a bonus if you suggested that continental areas are usually magmatically active for much longer than oceanic areas and also retain their magmatic heat for longer — this is Sclater's argument, which is summarized near the end of Section 2.1.2.)

(c) Pollack and Chapman used the geotherms shown in Figure 2.12, but placed the lithosphere–asthenosphere boundary at a temperature along the geotherm which is 85% of the dry solidus rather than at the adiabat. At deep levels (e.g. 200–300 km) the $0.85T_s$ temperature is considerably greater than the mantle adiabat temperature (see Figure 2.12 — at 200 km, the adiabat is at 1 400 °C, whereas $0.85T_s$ is 1 510 °C). This is the principal reason why the use of $0.85T_s$ overestimates lithosphere thicknesses at deep levels associated with low heat flow.

The second reason is more elusive and is related to Sclater's argument that heat flow from beneath the upper crustal radiothermal layer is greater than previously thought because the importance of radiothermal heating has been overestimated. A higher continental heat flow in the mantle will straighten the geotherms, leading to intersections with the mantle adiabat at slightly shallower depths than in Figure 2.12.

SAQ 2.5 (a), (c), (d) and (f) are true; (b) and (e) are false.

(a) The temperature at 10 km depth, from equation 2.4 will be

$$\Delta T = \frac{\overline{q}z}{k} = \frac{50 \times 10^{-3} \times 10 \times 10^{3}}{3.0} = 167\,^{\circ}\text{C}.$$

ΔT across the remainder of this fairly thick lithosphere will be $1\,350 - 167 = 1\,183\,^{\circ}\text{C}$.

$$z = \frac{k\Delta T}{q^*} = \frac{3.0 \times 1\,183}{30 \times 10^{-3}} = 118 \times 10^{3}\,\text{m or } 118\,\text{km}.$$

So the total thickness is $10 + 118 = 128$ km.

(b) It is the volcanic pipes themselves that are 90 Ma old; the lithospheric mantle itself equilibrated 3 200 Ma ago (Section 2.1.2) and the 40 mW m^{-2} geotherm is quite consistent with this age and implied lithosphere thickness.

(c) See Figure 2.15 and associated text.

(d) See Figure 2.16 and associated text.

(e) If the words elastic and plastic are interchanged, this statement will be true; remember that the whole Earth has *elastic* properties when the transmission of short-duration seismic waves is considered.

(f) See Figure 2.17 and the text at the end of Section 2.1.2.

SAQ 2.6 (a) When a shearing force is applied to crystalline material, elastic deformation describes the ability of the material to recover its original shape when the force is removed, whereas inelastic (or plastic) deformation leaves the material permanently deformed (cf. Figure 2.19).

(b) As emphasized in SAQ 2.5, the asthenosphere is defined as a layer that deforms permanently, therefore inelastically, whereas the low velocity zone behaves elastically, but with reduced elastic moduli compared with the surrounding mantle.

(c) The dynamic viscosity of a material is its ability to resist motion due to shearing stress. (More precisely, it is the shearing stress multiplied by the velocity gradient — Figure 2.18 — induced by that stress.) There is no hard and fast rule describing the relationship between elastic/inelastic deformation and dynamic viscosity because all materials have a finite viscosity. Quite simply, however, materials with a viscosity of 10^{24}–10^{25} Pa s tend to resist permanent deformation on geologically realistic time-scales, whereas those with viscosities of 10^{20}–10^{21} Pa s are more easily deformed permanently under the range of stresses available in the Earth.

SAQ 2.7 (a) Brittle deformation refers to the breaking and fracturing of rocks that occurs in the uppermost and coldest parts of the lithosphere when under stress; in general, this type of deformation occurs where laterally directed shearing stresses exceed vertical pressure due to the mass of overlying rocks.

(b) Ductile deformation, or ductile flow, occurs where the material of the lithosphere is sufficiently hot to yield inelastically under the prevailing stress regime. Higher temperature, higher stress magnitude, or greater time will all favour ductile deformation.

(c) Whole lithosphere failure refers to the condition whereby the prevailing stress on the lithosphere has been amplified, or focused on any remaining elastic regions (between the brittle layer above and ductile layers below) such that these elastic regions have reached the point of failure (Figure 2.20). At this point, the whole lithosphere will become permanently thinned (in extension) or thickened (in compression).

(d) The critical stress is the pressure across the lithosphere required to produce whole lithosphere failure in 1 Ma; it depends on the compositional profile of the lithosphere in question, the temperature gradient, and hence the heat flow.

SAQ 2.8 (a) The primary reason is that rocks are much stronger under compressional than extensional stress, and this is clearly shown by the critical stress required to produce whole lithosphere failure in Figure 2.24. Compressional deformation at high strain rates rapidly cools the lithosphere section (see transient geotherm, $t = 0$ in Figure 2.32), so strain hardening the lithosphere and causing it to resist deformation. Low strain rates lead to strain softening ($t = \infty$ in Figure 2.32) but, of course, take a great deal of time to achieve significant shortening. (See also ITQ 2.10.)

(b) The forces acting on lithospheric plates in general cause the whole plate to move, with ductile flow in the asthenosphere accommodating this motion. Only when there are resistive forces, or opposing forces acting to produce stress *within* a plate, does within-plate deformation occur. The highest magnitude stresses will therefore tend to occur at plate boundaries, where two plates with different overall stress regimes are in juxtaposition (see discussions in Sections 2.2.2 and 2.2.3).

(c) When topographic anomalies occur, for example mountains due to continental collision, they are isostatically compensated by deep crustal roots. These become hot, and are therefore more susceptible to ductile flow because of their lowered viscosity, and material moves sideways away from the anomalous zone (Figure 2.33). Gradually the mountains sink (and are eroded) as material is removed from beneath until thermal, viscous and isostatic equilibrium are re-established, with a crust equal in thickness to that surrounding the previously anomalous region.

SAQ 3.1 (a) The Antarctic Plate is entirely surrounded by spreading ridges, so, like the African Plate in ITQ 3.1, it must be growing progressively in size. Not all the plate movement vectors in Figure 3.3 are directed *towards* Antarctica itself, but the fact that there is no subduction boundary anywhere south of the ring of extensional ridges in the Indian, Pacific and Atlantic Oceans indicates that the deduction of a growing Antarctic Plate, with the ridges migrating north, is likely to be valid. Of course, the regions close to the Earth's south pole are greatly expanded by the projection used in Figure 3.3.

(b) The tectonic stress regime in New Zealand results from a combination of northwards movement from the circum-Antarctic ridge and westwards movement from the East Pacific Rise (the boundary between the Nazca and Pacific Plates). New Zealand is situated at the boundary of the Indian and Pacific Plates, where Pacific oceanic lithosphere is being subducted, but where there is strike–slip motion due to more rapid northwards movement west of the Indian–Pacific plate boundary. This is a transpressive plate boundary.

(c) A rather similar transpressive situation exists in the North Atlantic adjacent to the Mediterranean, where spreading from the equatorial zones is directed northeast, while that from north of the supposed convergent boundary is directed just south of east. Thus there is a degree of convergence coupled with strike–slip motion because of differences in the Atlantic spreading components directed parallel to this east–west boundary. We know that the Atlantic Ridge is migrating west in an absolute frame of reference, so the RRT triple junction at 20° W, 35° N must also be migrating to the west, *extending* the length of the transpressive boundary in question.

SAQ 3.2 Statements a, c, and d are true; b and e are false.

(a) See Section 3.2.1, also Figure 3.9, and note that back-arc spreading is thought to be related to frictional effects at the boundary between the overlying and down-going lithosphere, effects that induce asthenospheric convection, especially where convergence rates are rapid.

(b) At first sight, this might seem correct, but remember that we must define a fixed point in an absolute frame of reference. Certainly, a marginal basin undergoing back-arc spreading must grow in size, unless there is a second subduction zone and arc system on the landward side of the basin (e.g. the Ryukyu arc in Figure 3.8). But, as it grows, *either* the arc–trench system will be pushed out into the ocean basin, increasing the ocean–ocean